West Africa's Trouble Spots and the Imperative for Peace-Building

Osita Agbu

Monograph Series

The CODESRIA Monograph Series is published to stimulate debate, comments, and further research on the subjects covered. The Series serves as a forum for works based on the findings of original research, which however are too long for academic journals but not long enough to be published as books, and which deserve to be accessible to the research community in Africa and elsewhere. Such works may be case studies, theoretical debates or both, but they incorporate significant findings, analyses, and critical evaluations of the current literature on the subjects in question.

© Council for the Development of Social Science Research in Africa, 2006
Avenue Cheikh Anta Diop Angle Canal IV, BP 3304 Dakar, 18524, Senegal
Web site: www.codesria.org

Typeset by Daouda Thiam

Cover image designed by Ibrahima Fofana

Printed by Imprimerie Saint Paul, Dakar, Senegal

Distributed in Africa by CODESRIA

Distributed elsewhere by the African Books Collective
www.africanbookscollective.com

Monograph Series
ISBN: 2-86978-193-8

CODESRIA would like to express its gratitude to the Swedish International
Development Cooperation Agency (SIDA), the International Development
Research Centre (IDRC), Ford Foundation, MacArthur Foundation, Carnegie
Corporation, the Norwegian Ministry of Foreign Affairs, the Danish Agency for
International Development (DANIDA), the French Ministry of Cooperation, the
United Nations Development Programme (UNDP), the Netherlands Ministry of
Foreign Affairs, Rockefeller Foundation, FINIDA, NORAD, CIDA, IIEP/ADEA,
OECD, IFS, OXFAM America, UN/UNICEF and the Government of Senegal for
supporting its research, training and publication programmes

To Isaac Nwakor Agbu
For leaving us with a legacy of simplicity and thirst for knowledge

Contents

List of Abbreviations

AAFC	Allied Armed Forces of the Community
ACRI	African Crisis Response Initiative
AFL	Armed Forces of Liberia
AFRC	Armed Forces Ruling Council
ANAD	*Accord de Non Agression et d'Assistance en matière de Défense*
APC	Arewa Peoples Congress
AU	African Union
CAP	Children Assistance Programme
CEAO	*Communauté Economique de l'Afrique de l'Ouest*
CNE	*Commission Nationale Electorale*
CNSP	*Comité National du Salut Public*
CODESRIA	Council for the Development of Social Science Research in Africa
COMANET	Conflict Management Network
CPLP	*Communidade dos Paises de Lingua Portuguesa*
DDR	Disarmament, Demobilisation and Reintegration
DRC	Democratic Republic of Congo
ECOMOG	ECOWAS Ceasefire Monitoring Group
ECOWAS	Economic Community of West African States
EO	Executive Outcomes
EWARNET	Early Warning Network
FPI	*Front Populaire Ivoirien*
INPFL	Independent National Patriotic Front of Liberia
IRCSL	Inter-Religious Council of Sierra Leone
LURD	Liberians United for Reconciliation and Democracy
MASSOB	Movement for the Actualization of the Sovereign State of Biafra
MFDC	*Mouvement des Forces Démocratiques de la Casamance*
MISAB	Inter-African Stabilization Mission in Bangui
MODEL	Mandingo Organised for Democracy in Liberia (Movement for Democracy in Liberia)
MPCI	*Mouvement Patriotique de la Côte d'Ivoire*
MPIGO	*Mouvement Populaire Ivoirien du Grand Ouest*
MRU	Mano River Union
MSF	Médecins Sans Frontiers

NCCP	National Co-ordinating Committee for Peace
NIIA	Nigerian Institute of International Affairs
NPFL	National Patriotic Front of Liberia
OAU	Organisation of African Unity
ONUSAL	UN Observer Group to El Salvador
OPC	Oodua Peoples Congress
PCASED	Programme for Coordination and Assistance for Security and Development
PDCI	*Parti Démocratique de la Côte d'Ivoire*
PDP	Peoples Democratic Party
PMAD	Protocol on Mutual Assistance on Defence
PRONACO	Pro-National Conference Organization
PSO	Peace Support Operations
PSR	Party for Social Renewal
RDR	*Rassemblement des Républicains*
RECAMP	Reinforcement of African Capacity for Peace-Keeping
RUF	Revolutionary United Front
SLA	Sierra Leone Army
SLPP	Sierra Leone Peoples Party
SLWMP	Sierra Leone Women's Movement for Peace
SNC	Sovereign National Conference
ULIMO	United Liberian Movement for Democracy in Liberia
UNAMSIL	United Nations Mission in Sierra Leone
UNOMIL	United Nations Observer Mission in Liberia
UNOMSIL	United Nations Observer Mission in Sierra Leone
UNDP	United Nations Development Programme
UNESCO	United Nations Educational, Scientific and Cultural Organisation
UNICEF	United Nations International Children Emergency Fund
UNOGBIS	United Nations Peace Building Office in Guinea
UNOMIL	United Nations Observer Mission in Liberia
UNRISD	United Nations Research Institute for Social Development
WILPF	Women International League for Peace and Freetown
WMP	Women's Movement for Peace
WOMEN	Women Organised for a Morally Enlightened Nation

Foreword

This work is a comprehensive examination of the state of conflicts and the post-conflict environment in West Africa. It is outstanding in its analysis of the causes and interconnection between conflicts in the various trouble spots in the region. The monograph deals with the challenges of peace-building and is refreshing in its prescription of the need to effectively move away from traditional peacekeeping to the more durable peace-building strategy as the long-term solution for regional conflicts.

The study should be appreciated against the background of numerous conflicts of low-intensity and deadly dimensions going on in Africa. In West Africa, Côte d'Ivoire, Nigeria, Senegal, Niger, Guinea Bissau and Mauritania have the potential for violent crises and recurring conflicts and even wars. The failure of post-conflict resolution mechanisms makes it imperative to give serious thought to Osita Agbu's case in favour of regional peace-building as a sustainable solution to the conflicts in the West African region. I consider this monograph a major contribution to the literature on post-conflict peace-building. It is highly recommended as a worthy source of information.

Professor Adebayo Olukoshi
Executive Secretary
CODESRIA

Preface and Acknowledgement

This monograph is written with the intention to highlight the necessity for taking preventive measures in the form of peace-building as a sustainable and long-term solution to conflicts in the West African sub-region, with a special focus on the Mano River Union countries. Apart from the Mano River Union countries, efforts at resolving other conflicts in say, Guinea Bissau, Senegal/Casamance, Côte d'Ivoire and Nigeria have suffered from a lack of attention on the post-conflict imperatives of building peace in order to ensure that sustainable peace is achieved. Given the often intractable and inter-related nature of conflicts in this region, I argue for the need to revisit the existing mechanisms of conflict resolution in the sub-region with a view to canvassing a stronger case for stakeholders towards adopting the peace-building strategy as a more practical and sustainable way of avoiding wars in the sub-region.

Whether in Liberia, Sierra Leone, Guinea, Côte d'Ivoire or in Nigeria people desire long-lasting peace without which even minimal development is impossible. As conceptualised and presented in detail in this book, peace-building in consonance with its infrastructure is a more sustainable approach to ensuring regional peace and stability and, therefore, ensuring development for the peoples of West Africa.

I am greatly indebted to many who have contributed to what is written in this book: - scholars, statesmen, activists, libraries and Non-governmental organisations. In particular, I wish to acknowledge Ebrima Sall and other scholars at the Nordic Africa Institute, Uppsala; and my colleagues at the Nigerian Institute of International Affairs (NIIA), Lagos, in particular Cyril Obi, Charles Dokubo and S.B. Peters. I also, extend my appreciation to the two assessors who went through the manuscript for their incisive suggestions. Their comments went a long way in improving the quality of this book. Finally, I wish to acknowledge the financial contributions of the Council for the Development of Social Science Research in Africa (CODESRIA) in Senegal and the NIIA, Lagos for ensuring that this project is completed.

Osita Agbu
February 2005

1

Introduction

The various low-intensity and deadly conflicts going on in Africa have serious implications for development and it is imperative that long lasting solutions are sought. Given that these conflicts raged on and off for many years inthe West African sub-region, for example in Liberia, Sierra Leone and in the Casamance region of Senegal, it is time for African leaders and various stakeholders to begin designing sustainable solutions to these conflicts. It is to the Mano River Union (MRU) that this enquiry principally focuses on, though other parts of West Africa with long-standing or recurrent conflicts are also examined. The MRU was established in 1973 with the objective of achieving economic integration amongst the member countries of the Union. The Union aimed to establish a customs union amongst the member states, but, rather than achieving this aim, it has been bedevilled by intractable conflicts beginning from the early 1990s. Perhaps it is time to consider a long term solution to the situation, by designing peace-building initiatives and implementing these in a collaborative manner.

In West Africa, there have been alarming incidences of medium and high intensity conflicts with the attendant consequences of deaths, instability, displacements and refugees. This situation has given rise to serious breakdown of law and order in many societies, bringing in its wake immense insecurity and human suffering of grave dimensions, especially in Liberia, Sierra Leone, Guinea and even in Côte d'Ivoire. The fairly common view of many statesmen and scholars especially in the west, of cases of virtual state collapse and incapacity to engender development in Africa require that serious attention be focused on how to permanently address the incessant and unending civil wars in the sub-region as the situation has contributed significantly to Africa's inability to really embark on the path of development.

West Africa is indeed quite varied in terms of the political composition of countries in the sub-region. Note for instance, the differences in size, the differences in colonially inherited languages and norms, in levels of economic endowment and development, and the diversity of external linkages[1]. There are sixteen countries in West Africa, while nine are collectively referred to as Franco-phone; five are Anglophone and two Lusophone. However, Mauritania pulled out of the Economic Community of West African States (ECOWAS), the umbrella economic and political organization in the sub-region leaving fifteen countries. Such a mixture of colonial tutelage and experiences led to a situation in which diverse regional multilateral co-operation arrangements and institutions emerged after the independence period of the 1960s. The problem this has created in recent times is the difficulty of co-ordinating peace efforts and regional corporation in the region. The existing conflicts with roots in a multiplicity of factors- historical, political, economic as well as ecological/ environmental and ethnic/communal create and recreate contradictions and cleavages that have simply refused to recede or abate.

The 'Post-cold war' transition period has been significantly characterised by the drive towards democratisation on the one hand, and the re-emergence of ethnic nationalism on the other. Both of which have contributed significantly to exacerbating some of the low-intensity conflicts in the region, an example of which is the Nigerian case. This is neither to say that democracy is undesirable nor a justifiable end in itself.[2] Since the end of the cold war, conflicts have been increasingly intra-state rather than inter-state in nature. Oftentimes, these conflicts involve a very high level of brutality, mostly against civilians, and often by both conventional and unconventional forces, and methods.[3] Sometimes these conflicts spill across national borders, either in the form of combatants exporting the wars, or refugees seeking safe havens outside the theatre of war thus leading to sub-regional insecurity and, therefore demanding a sub- regional resolution effort rather than just a national solution. It is significant to note that of 82 medium to high intensity conflicts between 1992 and 1995 which involved the loss of at least 1000 lives, all but three were intra-state conflicts or civil wars.[4] Also, of a hundred armed conflicts around the world between 1990 and the year 2000, all but six occurred within states.[5]

There is little doubt that democratisation has in recent times created new opportunities as well as new uncertainties. These uncertainties have sometimes led to serious disputes. In some instances, like in Nigeria, democracy and democratisation have instead of releasing the necessary energies for development and the strengthening of the polity, resulted in a rather unbridled display of ethnic identity struggles. These struggles include jostling for ethnic advantages in accessing political offices as well as resource control rights. It is therefore, instructive to observe the relationship between democratisation and the increase in agitations for resource control. As expected, and in line with what has been observed elsewhere, namely in Ghana and Sierra Leone, these agitations have led to low-intensity conflicts, especially in Nigeria's Niger Delta area. Further, most of the wars in Africa have been fought over or are being fought over the control of mineral wealth like the civil wars in Liberia, Sierra Leone, Angola and the Democratic Republic of Congo (DRC). The implication of this is that the Post-colonial state in Africa is seen as being increasingly attractive as a source of 'mining' public resources. It also means that these conflicts tend to quickly exacerbate affecting civilian populations in ways that were not so before. As Hyden[6] noted, African conflicts are typically over resources rather than identity; they are usually triggered off by competitive politics associated with the election systems but invariably take on cultural and ethnic dimensions.

Though, various methods of conflict management and resolution, both formal and informal have been used in trying to resolve some of Africa's intractable conflicts, the results have not been satisfactory. Sudan, Somalia and the Democratic Republic of Congo (DRC) remain cases in point. Instead of the conflicts being finally resolved what is often more common is some kind of resurgence. This means that there maybe something wrong with the approaches so far applied in addressing these conflicts. This is not, however, to ignore the fact that the particular forms of tensions generated by 'new wars' and their specific characteristics may also have made resolution difficult. By 'new wars', we mean wars like the Sierra Leone civil war, where conflicts are characterized by struggles between armed factions that contend for resources amidst the collapse of state institutions, rather than mass-based political movements that fight to promote particular visions or ideologies. Recognising the apparent shortcomings in the conflict resolution efforts, the United Nations has in recent times resorted to the use of Peace Support Operations (PSOs) in instances where this is applicable. Even at this, since 1995 only three UN PSOs have been mandated in contrast to over forty years of the use of interpositioning logic as the mode of peacekeeping,[7] i.e. deploying UN peacekeepers between the conflicting parties in order to achieve a cease-fire, after which further negotiations for settlement continue. Generally recognised therefore, is the need for the longer-term task of reconstruction and reconciliation, sometimes referred to as peace-building as an alternative strategy both for addressing the post-war demands of conflicts and building a basis for containing future conflicts. Here, there is logically the necessity for ensuring human security which is very important considering the weak nature of political and economic institutions in Africa.[8] There is indeed growing consensus that a regional approach to seeking solutions to the kinds of conflicts that exist in Africa will be a more effective and sustainable strategy. This is in tandem with the observation by Adeniji,[9] that global security in the Post-war world compels each state to conceive its security and stability as being closely linked with those of its neighbours. In fact, Barry Buzan originally presented this perspective as 'security complexes'. This now leads us towards presenting a theoretical foundation for the idea being canvassed in this study. And this is the idea of managing conflicts in the West African sub-region through a focus on regional peace-building measures. By sub-region, is meant a focus on the geographical space known as West Africa, that is characterized by interactions between various actors and institutions. A key feature here being the cooperation between the states in the territory.

Barry Buzan introduced a discourse on the security concept in *People, States and Fear*[10] where he problematized both the realist and liberal approaches to understanding security. For him, as a system model, the balance of power theory offers no more enlightenment on national security problem than do other power structure models. He argues for a perspective on security that goes beyond the questions of power and peace. In extending the discussion on security, Buzan argues that the security concept itself provides an important analytical approach to the understanding of behaviour. Accordingly, Buzan defines the security complex as a group of states whose primary security concerns are linked together sufficiently closely that their national securities cannot realistically be considered apart from one another.[11] The mutual feeling of a high level of threat among two or more states in a region is the key factor in motivating a collective action. This idea of the security complex was further developed by Barry Buzan, Jaap de Wilde and Ole Weaver in 'Security: a New framework for Analysis, with the introduction of a sectoral perspective to the security complex theory'. In elaborating a sector approach to security, Barry Buzan et al. sees security as consisting of five sectors: military, political, societal, economic, and ecological.[12]

In explicating the security complex theory, Buzan cited the India-Pakistan conflict over Kashmir, pointing out that South Asia as a whole provides a relatively clear example of an important, middle level security by complex. He observes that what binds the South Asian security complex together is the dominant role of local issues and relations in defining the national security priorities of the states within it. For Buzan, security complexes are a typical product of an anarchic international structure, which closely reflects the operating environment of national security policy-makers than do higher-level abstractions about the distribution of power in the system. In his understanding, almost every country will be able to relate its security perspectives to one or more complexes. Hence, the concept provides a useful tool for organising patterns of relations, and for arranging them into lateral and hierarchical categories.[13]

Analytically, security complexes offer an approach to security, which requires attention to both the macro-level of great power impact on the system, and the micro-level of local state relations. In drawing attention to both levels, security complexes emphasize the mutuality of impact between them, with external influences tending to amplify local problems, and local problems shaping and constraining external entanglements and influences.[14] Generally, security complexes can be used as either static or a dynamic mode of analysis. As a static framework, the idea generates a perspective and a set of questions that can be applied to any situational analysis. As a dynamic framework, security complexes offer a class of durable entities whose patterns and processes of evolution are of as much theoretical, and perhaps more practical interest as those of the power structures of the system as a whole.[15] It is from this angle that this study extrapolates from the basic features of security complexes in applying its analytical usefulness to exploring possibilities of enhancing human security through regional peace-building in the mode of 'security community'[15] rather than just state-centered measures at peace-building.

It is in this light that a reconceptualization of African security away from the usual focus on state control or preoccupation with regime stability is fundamental. This re-focusing could greatly reduce citizen alienation from the state while creating a benign attitude to social and political development. Hence, the alternative strategy to addressing conflicts in Africa is to focus as much as possible on preventive diplomacy, peacemaking and peace-building. Peace-building invariably becomes a mechanism for achieving human security in an environment that is bedevilled by insecurity as a result of unmitigated conflicts.

Generally, peace-building as a strategy is all-embracing and leaves little room for the exclusion of parties or interests to conflicts,[16] the proposition being that there is the need for any conflict resolution mechanism to focus more on post-conflict reconstruction, reconciliation and peace-building, which no doubt has a long-term impact. The expectation is that this process will develop simultaneously a culture of peace as opposed to that of aggression and violence in the West African sub-region. Peace-building, which entails thinking positively about conflicts and consciously building peace or harmony, is basically peace in action. It has been described as the power generated by the interactive triangle of peace, development and democracy.[17] It highlights and assists people to be able to live together. In this wise, focus on post-conflict rehabilitation, democracy and growth of civil society institutions, demilitarisation and rehabilitation, peace education and a myriad of other short and long-term measures become imperative.

Review of the Causes and Nature of Conflicts in Africa

Generally, scholars agree that conflict represents part of the inevitable dynamics of human relations.[18] According to Imobighe,[19] to satisfy their needs, human beings must of necessity interact with, and in the process make demands on their environment, their society and fellow human beings. In the process of such interactions, conflict could arise due to the incompatibility of the goals they pursue, or incompatibility of the means they use in pursuing their chosen goals. Oftentimes, it is difficult to establish the precise causes of conflicts largely because conflicts differ from each other in terms of the combination of factors that give rise to them, and also because conflicts are social phenomena involving human beings and are not necessarily given to rigid scientific explanations. Stedman[20] has for example, observed that crises and conflicts in Africa, especially at the national and sub-national levels, couldbe seen to revolve around the four important issues of identity, participation, distribution and legitimacy. Another school of thought sees economic decline as strongly associated with violent conflicts. The argument being that the nature of politics associated with a dwindling economy tends to be more ferocious than that associated with an economy that is growing or buoyant. Further, the process of political transitions to democracy in the continent has also been identified as providing a conducive environment for the eruption of conflicts.[21]

It is interesting to note that International Alert, one of the NGOs at the forefront of the efforts at peace-building in West Africa, observed that no one state in the region can be exempted from having suffered from conflict. However, it identifies four main conflict areas in the region: the Mano River Union (MRU), constituting Liberia, Sierra Leone and Guinea-Conakry, and Côte d'Ivoire, which relates closely to the MRU conflict; Senegal and Guinea-Bissau; Mali and Niger; and Nigeria, whose conflicts are for now self-contained.[22] According to International Alert, conflicts in the region are expressed as the ethnicisation of politics; the use of religion as a means of mobilisation; the violent assertion of rights to self-determination; the collapse or near collapse of the state; resource conflicts and criminality through the trading of diamonds, oil and other precious minerals, arms, people and drugs in parallel markets. It sees structural causes of conflict in the region embodied in political legacies and economic prescriptions as being exacerbated by politics of exclusion coupled with assimilationist policies that seek to suppress group identities.[23] The literature is indeed rich in terms of the various views on the causes and character of conflicts in Africa, and West Africa in particular. For example, Joseph,[24] Nwokedi,[25] Young,[26] and Peters[27] analysed the causes of African conflicts by examining the character of the African State perceived as instrumental in fanning the embers of violence. Others like Yassim El-Ayouty[28] and Adetula[29] categorised African conflicts into major groups comprising boundary/territorial disputes, civil wars, colonial/racial wars, succession conflicts and political/ideological conflicts. Also, Bassey[30] identified some of the causes of conflicts as those pertaining to pressures of decolonization, widespread irredentism, civil disorder, vigilantism, coercive warfare and the diplomacy of violence. Some others see conflicts in West Africa as characterized by the machinations of warlords who battle 'strongmen' and 'political entrepreneurs' for control over mineral resources and access to markets against the increasing weakening of the neo-patrimonial state in Africa.[31] Some explanations of the root causes of conflict in Africa include the apocalyptic view,[32] the culturalist view,[33] neo-patrimonialism and civil wars,[34] and rational civil wars.[35] Whilst discussing all these is presently beyond my focus, it is important that we examine the economic perspective to wars in Africa.

Collier,[36] Grossman,[37] and Davies[38] examined the economic dimension of civil wars in Africa. Generally, the observation is that the risk of having increases in rebellion coincides with the opportunity for financing the rebellion, while it decreases with the level of rebel expenditure and the differential cost vis-à-vis government expenditure. The literature has also basically indicated three identifiable sources of rebel finance, as consisting of proceeds from extortion, donations from diaspora and subventions from hostile governments. Best,[39] Duffield,[40] and Mutisya[41] have studied other dimensions of conflict in the developing world, with Mutisya attributing the frequency of these conflicts to the phenomenon of failed states. Duffield noted for example, that the paradox of globalization lies in the prevalence of assumptions linking economic convergence with social and political order, while countervailing divisions and disorder capable of causing conflicts are being forcefully reproduced on the ground. However, this view has been critiqued by scholars who feel that the economic explanations for wars in Africa tended to be simplistic and underplayed the importance of the historical and political factors. For instance, in an article written in 2002, Thandika Mkandawire[42] pointed out that the recent focus on the means of financing rebel movements and the failure of most movements to coherently articulate, let alone achieve, their proclaimed objectives have encouraged an easy dismissal of the politics of such movements and an inclination towards economistic, culturalist and militaristic interpretations of conflicts. He argues that to understand the actions of rebel movements and their violence in Africa, we must understand not only the elites and the intra-elite conflicts that produce their leaders, but also the actions and responses of the wider population.[43] Generally, Mkandawire makes the point that while economic explanations for the causes of war is important, it is not necessarily the cause of wars; secondly, that structural conditions that are propitious to insurgency, and the agency of individuals and social movements are important to understanding the terrible toll of rebel movements; and finally, that incoherent as the rebels' objectives may sound, they reflect a serious urban malaise that should not be lightly dismissed by reducing the members of these movements to simple criminals. He maintains that understanding the root causes of these conflicts is important for their resolution. This view cannot, but be more rational than simply criminalizing all conflicts in Africa.

Shortcomings relating to the inadequacies of the existing conflict resolution and management strategies have also been identified, and possible ways for improvement recommended. For example, Williams,[44] Bassey[45] and Vogts,[46] have all in their various contributions identified these shortcomings, with Vogts noting the formation in 1993 of the Mechanism for Conflict Prevention, Management and Resolution of Conflicts by the OAU; which even though it superseded the previous commission on Mediation, Arbitration and Conciliation did not achieve much. However, with the formation of African Union (AU) in 2000 as successor to the AU, it now has a Peace and Security Council (PSC), a body expected to oversee the implementation of efforts at ensuring peace in Africa. The success of this Council may invariably be determined by the availability of funds for its operations. Already the crisis in the Darfur region of Sudan, which warranted the deployment of AU peacekeepers from Nigeria and Rwanda in 2004, is tasking the capacity of the newly formed PSC. The Council was not initially able to muster enough troops to police the very wide expanse of land in and around Darfur.

On post-conflict peace-building, many have noted the necessity to explore this dimension as a sustainable strategy for managing conflicts. According to Akindele,[47] in an increasingly interdependent world, peace like war have become absolutely indivisible, meaning that there is a need to focus more on seeking peaceful co-existence and on building the peace . Hence, Boutros Boutros-Ghali,[48] and the United Nations Research Institute for Social Development (UNRISD) [49] have tried to popularize this strategy of conflict management. For instance, Boutros-Ghali suggested that for peace-making and peacekeeping operations to be truly successful they must include comprehensive efforts to identify and support structures which will tend to consolidate peace and advance a sense of confidence and well being amongst the people. UNRISD even identified five dimensions, along which the process of post-conflict rebuilding must be pursued, classifying these as political rebuilding, social rebuilding, psychological rebuilding, judicial rebuilding and economic rebuilding. Others like Sklar,[50] Hubert,[51] the UNDP[52] and UNESCO[53] highlighted the necessity for democracy, human rights, and building a culture of peace in seeking solutions to conflicts in Africa. Also Namadi[54] and Hay[55] highlighted the individual and group dimensions of peace building. Namadi for instance, conceives of peace-building as the constructing of positive and constructive perceptions of conflicts in the minds of the people. This could be done, he maintained, by initially making conscious efforts to transform attitudes through a generational orientation, which should begin with the individual. Hay, in the same contribution sees the overarching goal of peace-building as the enhancement of the indigenous capacity of a society to manage conflict without violence. To him, ultimately, peace-building should aim at building human security, a concept that includes democratic governance, human rights, rule of law, sustainable development, and equitable access to resources. Issues dealing with the peace concept and peace-building will be examined in the next chapter.

Though many recognised the need for this sort of approach (sustainable resolution of conflicts through peace-building measures), little has been done in terms of undertaking either a post-conflict evaluation of peace-building measures so far or a comparative examination of such efforts in a particular region. This study does so by focusing on the West African sub-region. The intricate and intertwining nature of conflicts in this region provides us with a good case study to assess the approaches so far attempted in building peace and the potential strategies that may further be adopted.

In introducing the subject matter, the object has been to paint a picture of the dimensions and facets of conflict in Africa generally, and West Africa in particular. In this section, the various views and sometimes critiques of the nature, character and categorizations of conflict in Africa have been presented with a view to providing a holistic understanding of the range of issues involved, and that may also be focused on in examining the case studies from West Africa. The expectation is that the rather comprehensive theoretical review will serve to broaden our articulation of possible solutions especially in relation to regional peace-building as a strategy.

Notes

1. Olu Adeniji, 'Mechanism for Conflict Prevention in West Africa: Politics of Harmonization', *ACCORD*, Occasional paper, 2/97, 1997.
2. J. Andrew Slack and Roy R. Doyon, 'Population Dynamics and Susceptibility for Ethnic Conflict: The Case of Bosnia and Herzegovina', *Journal of Peace Research*, Vol. 38, No., 2001.
3. Luca Renda, 'Ending Civil Wars: The Case of Liberia', *The Fletcher Forum of World Affairs*, Vol. 23: 2, 1999, p.59.
4. Philip Wilkinson, 'Sharpening the Weapons of Peace Support Operations and Complex Emergencies', *Peace Keeping and Conflict Resolution*, 1998, p.64.
5. Goran Hyden, 'Post-War Reconstruction and Democratization: Concepts, Goals and Lessons Learnt', Paper prepared for the seminar on 'After war: Reconciliation and Democratization in Divided Societies', Solstrand, 27-29 March 2000, p.2.
6. Hyden, ibid. p.2. See Also, William Reno, Review by John Hirsch, *Sierra Leone: Diamonds and the Struggle for Democracy*, London, International Peace Academy Occasional Papers Series and Boulder Co., Lynne Rienner Publishers, 2001, p.175.
7. Robin Hay, *Peace-Building during Peace Support Operation: A Survey and Analysis of Recent Mission*, Department of Foreign Affairs and International Trade, Canada, 1999.
8. NIIA, Communiqué of the Regional Conference on 'The Management of African Security in The 21st Century', Nigerian Institute of International Affairs, Lagos, Nigeria, 23-24 June, 1999.
9. Olu Adeniji, op cit. p.12.
10. Barry Buzan, *People, States and Fear: The National Security Problem in International Relations*, Sussex, Wheatsheaf Books Ltd., 1983.
11. Ibid. p.106.
12. Barry Buzan, Ole Waever, Jaap de Wilde (eds.), *Security: A New Framework for Analysis*, Boulder and London, Lynne Rienner, 1998.
13. Buzan, op cit. p.111.
14. Ibid. p. 12
15. Karl W. Deutsch, *Political Community and the North Atlantic Area: International Organizations in the Light of Historical Experience*, Princeton, Princeton University press, 1957.
16. F. Hampson, 'Building a Stable Peace: Opportunities and Limits to Security in Third World Regional Conflicts', *International Journal*, XLV, 2, spring 1990, p.477.
17. UNESCO, 'Global Movement for a Culture of Peace and Non-Violence', CAB-WS/ 4, 1999. See also, Osita Agbu, 'Democratization of Education for Refugees and Displaced Persons', Layi Erinosho et al., *Perspectives on Education For Tolerance and a Culture of Peace in Africa*, Federal Ministry of Education, Nigerian National Commission for UNESCO, Abuja, 2000.
18. John Burton, *World Society*, Lanham, University Press of America, 1987, pp.137-138. Also, Dudley Weeks, *The Eight Essential Steps to Conflict Resolution*, New York, Tarcher/Putman, 1992, p.ix.
19. Thomas A. Imobighe, 'Exploring the Conflict Management Potentials and Capacity of the AU Peace and Security Council', Paper presented at the one day National

Conference on the African Union and the Future of the African Continent, Nigerian Institute of International Affairs, Lagos, January 13, 2005.

20. Stephen Stedman, 'Conflict and Conflict Resolution in Africa: A Conceptual Framework', Francis Deng and I. William Zartman (eds.), *Conflict Resolution in Africa*, Washington D.C, The Brookings Institute, 1991, pp.374-383.

21. Ogaba Oche, 'The Commonwealth and the Imperatives of Conflict Management and Human Security', *Nigerian Journal of International Affairs*, Vol. 30, No.2, 2004, p.70.

22. International Alert, Strategising for Peace and Social Justice in West Africa: An Overview of West Africa Programme, 2004. Internet Site: http://www.international-alert.org/pdf/pubwestafrica/WA_overview_1_4.pdf. Visited 1 March 2005.

23. Ibid.

24. Richard Joseph, *Democracy and Prebendal Politics in Nigeria: The Rise and Fall of the Second Republic*, Cambridge, Cambridge University Press, 1987, p.181.

25. Emeka Nwokedi, 'African Security: Issues and Problems in the 1990s to the Next Millennium', Margaret Vogt and L.S. Aminu (eds), *Peace-Keeping as a Security Strategy in Africa: Chad and Liberia as Case Studies*, Enugu, Fourth Dimension Publishers, 1996, p.29.

26. Crawford Young, 'The African Colonial State and Its Political Legacy', in D. Rothschild and N. Chazan (eds.), *The Precarious Balance: The State and Security in Africa*, Boulder, Colorado: Westview Press, 1988, p.26.

27. Jimi Peters, 'The Nature of African Conflicts', Paper presented at the Regional Conference on the Management of African Security in the 21st Century, Nigerian Institute of International Affairs, Lagos, 23-24 June, 1999.

28. Yassim El-Ayouty and William Zartman (eds.), *The OAU After Twenty Years*, New York, Preager Publishers, 1984, p.103.

29. Victor Adetula, 'ECOWAS and the Liberian Crisis: An Approach in Conflict Management', *Nigerian Forum*, Vol.12, Nos.9-12, September–December, 1992.

30. Celestine Bassey, 'Nigeria and Regional Security in the West African Sub-Region: Lessons from Monrovia', *Nigerian Forum*, Vol.14, Nos.1 & 2, January-February 1994.

31. W. Reno, *Warlord Politics and African States*, Boulder CO., Lynne Rienner, 1998. Also, P. Richards, *Fighting for the Rainforest: War, Youth and Resources in Sierra Leone*, London, James Currey.

32. H.M Enzenberger, *Inbordeskrig*, Stockholm, Norstedts Storpocket, 1993.

33. Stephen Ellis, 'Liberia's Warlord Insurgency', in C. Clapham (ed.), *African Guerrillas*, Oxford, James Currey, 1998.

34. M. Bratton and N. Van de Walle, 'Neopatrimonial Regimes and Political Transitions in Africa', in P. Lewis (ed.), *Africa: the Dilemmas of Development and Change*, Boulder Co., Westview, 1998.

35. David Keen, 'The Political Economy of War', Workshop on Economic and Social Consequences of Conflicts, Queen Elizabeth House, University of Oxford, 1998.

36. P. Collier, 'Doing Well Out of War', in M. Berdal and D.M. Malone (eds.), *Greed and Grievance: Economic Agenda in Civil Wars*, Boulder and London, 2000.

37. H.I. Grossman, 'Kleptocracy and Revolutions', *Oxford Economic Papers*, 51, 1991, pp. 267-83.

38. Victor A.B. Davies, 'The Political Economy of African Civil Wars', Paper presented at the 13ᵗʰ Biennial Congress of the African Association of Political Science, Yaounde, Cameroun, June 19-22, 2001.

39. Shedrack G. Best, 'The Underdeveloped State of Peace and Conflict Studies in Africa', *African Peace Review*, Vol.2, No.1, April 1998, p.2.

40. Mark Duffield, 'Globalization and War Economies: Promoting Order or the Return of History', *The Fletcher Forum of World Affairs*, Vol.23, No.2, Fall, 1999, p.24.

41. Godfrey Mutisya, 'Conflict Watch', *Conflict Trends*, No.5, October 1998, p.9.

43. Ibid.p.182.

44. I.O. Williams, 'Analysis of Alternative Strategies for Africa in the 1990s and Beyond an African Deterrent Force', in Vogt and Aminu (eds.), *Peacekeeping as a Security Strategy in Africa: Chad and Liberia as Case Studies*, op cit., p.455.

45. Celestine Bassey, 'Alternative Models for Peacekeeping in Africa: A Sub-Regional Model', in Vogt and Aminu (eds.), *Peacekeeping as a Security Strategy in Africa: Chad and Liberia as Case Studies*, op cit. p.472.

46. Margaret Vogt, 'The Management of Conflicts in Africa', op cit. p.46.

47. R.A. Akindele, 'Conflict Theory, Conflict Behaviour and Conflict Control in the International System: A Theoretical Survey and Analysis', *Nigerian Journal of International Affairs*, Vol.13, No.1, 1987.

48. Boutros Boutros-Ghali, 'An Agenda for Peace: Preventive Diplomacy, Peace-Making and Peacekeeping', *Stockholm International Peace Research Institute Yearbook, 1993*, Oxford, Oxford University Press, 1995.

49. UNRISD, *States of Disarray: The Social Effects of Globalization*, Geneva, 1995, pp.120-121.

50. R.L. Sklar, 'Peace Through Freedom: The Resolution of International Conflict in Sub-Saharan Africa', Paper presented at the International Conference on Regional Conflict and Diplomatic Initiatives, Nigerian Institute of International Affairs, Lagos, Nigeria, 12-31, October, 1991, pp.13-14.

51. Don Hubert, 'Human Security: Safety for People in a Changing World', A Paper presented at the Two-Day Regional Conference on the *Management of African Security and Challenges of the 21ˢᵗ Century*, Nigerian Institute of International Affairs and the Canadian High Commission, Lagos, June 23-24, 1999.

52. UNDP, Human Development Report, Geneva, 1994; also, UNDP, 'Globalization with a Human Face', *Human Development Report*, Geneva, 1999.

53. UNESCO, 2000, op cit.

54. Mohammed Mustapha Namadi, 'The Concept of Peace Culture and Education for Peace Building', Paper presented at the Sub-Regional Seminar on the *Perspectives of Peace Education as a Basis for Achieving as Culture of Peace in Africa*, Nigerian National Commission for UNESCO, August 15-17, Abuja, 2000.

55. Robin Hay, 1999, op.cit.

2

Peace Concept and Peace-building

One cannot really discuss peace without talking about war. However, there is the need to consciously work at promoting or building peace after hostilities which involves a lot of activities geared towards not only returning to a state of normalcy but also, ensuring that future hostilities do not arise. Building a culture of peace implies trying to put in place the universal values of respect for life, liberty, justice, solidarity, human rights and equality between men and women. It entails changing value systems, attitudes and behaviours of peoples, especially in potentially explosive environments and relationships. Peace is therefore, an attitude; it is a way of life that should be cultivated.[1] Ordinarily, peace cannot be imposed on warring societies but must be a shared desire sincerely committed to by the parties in conflict if any effort at reconciliation is to stand any reasonable chance of success.

It has often been said that understanding peace is the first step to achieving it. This notwithstanding, even experts in peace studies do not have one accepted definition for the concept of peace. Some say, it is the absence of war. Others describe it as a situation that arises any time people address injustices and oppression. Still others see it in terms of peacemaking, that is, developing peace through human development, liberation and fulfilment.[2]

Further highlighting the inherent difficulty in understanding the concept, Sigmund Freud had observed in a letter to Albert Einstein that: 'conflict of interests among mankind is in the main, usually decided by the use of force. This is true of the whole animal kingdom from which mankind should not be excluded'.[3]

Though, it is not strange that the basis of survival is struggle, and that people must struggle for existence, what is however, strange is that even after attaining the maximum security, people still cannot live peacefully. It therefore, appears that peace is a rare phenomenon, and the challenge is even more demanding than war.[4]

There is now increasing evidence in support of the view that the culture of a society may have determining effects on interpersonal and inter-group relations within a society which may have implications for conflict and conflict resolution. The norms, values and traditions of a society may indeed have an impact on the state of peace in a particular society. The propensity for conflict within the society as well as the tendency to engage in violent confrontations with other societies, does not evolve from a vacuum, but is the product or rather a reflection of how that society has been shaping the mores and beliefs of its population.[5] Creating a culture of peace can be construed as creating a normal standard of behaviour that favours the peaceful resolution of conflicts, and one that stigmatises the use of violence, by any part of the society.[6] Peace, in one word stability, is the ultimate end usually desired by civilised peoples without which development is impossible. It is a means to an end and an end in itself for all. The examples of this are rife for those who care to search. Switzerland, Sweden and Japan invested heavily in peace and as the 21st century dawned, they are evidently enjoying the dividends of peace. This is attested to by the level of development in these countries, the peaceful co-existence, and of course, the quality of life of their citizens. On the other hand, many post-colonial states in Africa have for long been embroiled in all kinds of civil wars and coups d'état, from boundary wars to economic wars, and the price they have had to pay for these is quite high. This is the near absolute lack of development in almost all reasonable areas of human development. In fact, many of the states in Africa, are increasingly being perceived as collapsed or failing states.[7]

As opposed to peace and the dividends derivable from peace, conflict in its most literal sense disorganises a society, and renders it incapable of embarking on the natural part to development. Serious disputes, disagreements, confrontation, struggles or battles that could be violent or non-violent usually accompany it. Akindele,[8] aptly defined conflict as a situation of competition in which the parties are aware of the incompatibility of potential future positions and in which each party wishes to occupy a position that is incompatible with the wishes of the other. The key word here is incompatibility, and that was also reflected in the definition given by Dougherty and Pfaltzgraf.[9] Both understood conflict as a condition in which one identifiable group of human beings (whether tribal, ethnic, cultural, religious, socio-economic, political or other) is engaged in conscious opposition to one or more other identifiable groups because these groups are pursuing what are or appear to be *incompatible* goals. Therefore, the essence of peace and a culture of peace is being able to develop the disposition and thus, the mechanisms for managing the incompatibilities between competing parties in a society before these differences turn violent.

On peacekeeping as a conflict resolution mechanism, the explanations given by Nkiwane[10] are poignant and clear. According to her, peacekeeping in its traditional sense is simply the deployment of military and sometimes civilian personnel under international command and control, usually after a cease-fire has been achieved and with the consent of the parties involved. Whilst peacekeeping is a military third intervention to assist parties in transition from violent to sustainable peace, peacemaking on the other hand, is the diplomatic effort to end the violence between conflicting parties, move to a stage of non-violent dialogue, and eventually reach a peace agreement. Peacekeeping requires the consent of all parties, and a reasonable level of impartiality. It is not intended to alter the balance of power, but rather to interpose forces in order to develop an enabling environment for peacekeeping efforts to be established or re-established. Peacekeeping also operates under the principle of non-use of force, except in self-defense. In this wise, UN Observer Missions are generally unarmed, however, the increasingly violent and senseless acts of armed parties to conflicts around the world, as was the case during the Bosnian conflict and the civil wars in Liberia and Sierra Leone sometimes forced peacekeepers to become peace-enforcers.

Related to peacekeeping, and an incremental development in the United Nations repertoire of field experience is what has come to be known as Peace Support Operations (PSOs). This is a term used by the military to cover both peace-keeping and peace enforcement operations, but is now used more widely to embrace in addition, those other peace-related operations which include conflict prevention, peacemaking, peace-building and humanitarian assistance.[11]

Peace-building in particular, is a fairly new concept and an even newer field of study.[12] Students of international affairs agree that it was the dismantling of the Berlin wall in 1989 – a symbol of a dangerously divided world – that gave the international community the opportunity to view peace not simply as the preservation of the precarious balance of power among competing blocs, but as an ongoing concern for human security in a rapidly changing global system.[13]

On post-conflict peace-building which some like Johan Galtung[14] prefer to understand as post-settlement peace-building, the object is to first, perform the negative task of preventing a relapse into overt violence, while secondly, performing the positive task of aiding national recovery and eventual removal of the underlying causes of internal war. It was the former United Nations (UN) Secretary General, Boutros Boutros Ghali who gave political currency to the concept of peace-building when he submitted his Report, *An Agenda for Peace*, to the 47th Session of the UN on 17 June 1992. In the 1992 *Agenda for Peace*, Post-conflict peace-building was defined as 'actions to identify and support structures which will tend to strengthen and solidify peace in order to avoid a relapse into conflict'.[15] In a supplement to *An Agenda for Peace*, the key elements to peace-building were described in expanded terms in paragraph 47 as consisting of demilitarisation, the control of small arms, institutional reforms, improved Police and Judicial systems, the monitoring of Human Rights, electoral reform, and social and economic development. By 1997, post-conflict peace-building was seen to involve 'the creation or strengthening of national institutions, the monitoring of elections, the promotion of Human Rights, the provision of reintegration and rehabilitation programmes and the creation of conditions for resumed development.[16] While Kumar,[17] sees peace-building as involving a self-sustaining process for the pre-emptive management of disputes, Evans,[18] defines it as a set of strategies which aim to ensure that disputes, armed conflicts and other major crises do not arise in the first place – and when they do arise – that they do not subsequently recur. The most striking feature of the peace-building concept is its utility for the future. It goes beyond just peacekeeping and peacemaking to embrace measures designed to ensure that there is stability in the future.

It is basically a process that facilitates the establishment of durable peace and tries to prevent the recurrence of conflicts by addressing root causes and effects through reconciliation, institution building, and political as well as economic transformation.[19] Peace-building initiatives try to fix the core problems that underlie a conflict and change the pattern of interaction of the involved parties.[20] The essence being to transform relationships from that of a condition of extreme vulnerability and dependency to one of self-sufficiency and well being.[21] A distinction could be drawn between post-conflict peace-building and long-term peace-building. Post-conflict peace-building is connected to peacekeeping, and often involves demobilization and reintegration programmes, as well as reconciliation needs. However, while peacemaking and peacekeeping are important parts of peace transitions, they are not adequate in meeting the longer-term imperative of building a lasting peace. Long-term peace-building techniques are therefore designed to fill this gap, and address underlying substantive issues to the conflict. This is crucial to future violence prevention, and the promotion of a more peaceful future.[22]

There is also a structural dimension to peace-building which focuses on the social conditions that foster violent conflict. This implies that peace must be built on social, economic and political foundations that serve the needs of the populace. For instance, the promotion of substantive and procedural justice through structural means typically involves institution building and the strengthening of civil society. In addition, strong executive, legislative and judicial institutions are necessary to be able to deliver services to the people. In other words, democratization is a key instrument in creating peace enhancement structures. So, post-conflict peace-building should be a part of the comprehensive project to rebuild society's institutions. Usually, political structural changes focus on political development, state building, and the establishment of effective governance institutions. These often involve election reform, judicial reform, power-sharing initiatives, constitution reform, building political parties, creating conflict resolution institutions, and establishing mechanisms to monitor and protect human rights.

Further, structural changes could also be economic. This is because economic development is integral to preventing future conflict and avoiding a relapse into violence.[23] Some economic factors that put society at risk include lack of employment opportunities, scarcity, and lack of access to natural resources or land. Economic peace-building measures should be targeted at both micro- and macro- levels in order to be able to create opportunities that will benefit the populace.

An integral aspect of peace-building is to reduce the war-related hostility through repair and transformation of damaged relationships. This focuses on reconciliation, forgiveness, trust building and future imaging,[24] and seeks to minimize poorly functioning communication and maximize mutual understanding.[25] At the grassroots level, effective communication and negotiation is necessary for the transformation of conflicts. This ideally enhances dialogue, which helps to increase awareness of the other party's interests and identity, and therefore ensures proper future imaging. Future imaging is a situation in which parties to a conflict are able to form a vision of a commonly shared future that they wish to build. This is possible because conflicting parties often have more in common of their visions of the future than they do of their shared and violent past.[26]

Another dimension to peace-building according to Paul Lederach is the personal dimension. This centres on desired changes at the individual level considered necessary in the sustainable resolution of conflicts. If individuals do not go through a process of healing, there may arise broader social, political and economic repercussions. It is important that reconciliation efforts involve the treatment of mentally traumatized persons. This is because when the social psychology of a conflict and its consequences are left unattended to, this is likely to lead to certain risks for the society. Indeed, traumatized victims may become perpetrators of violent crimes in the future. In all these efforts, is the role expected to be played by peace-building agents including the civil society, people in leadership positions, the religious leaders, and others at the grassroots level. This is necessary because peace-building measures involve many actors at different levels in the society and also, targets all aspects of the state structure.

It is believed that the greatest resource for sustaining peace in the long term is the local people and their culture. It is always important to try and understand the cultural dimension of a conflict, and if possible identify the mechanisms for resolving conflict that exist within that cultural setting. Even peoples of war-torn Liberia had such mechanisms in the past. For example, the Kpelle people of Liberia had a well-established forum for informal settlement of conflicts. It was called the 'House of Palaver' or 'moot', which was made up of an ad hoc council of kinsmen and neighbours of parties in conflict. Usually, claims were investigated with honesty, and at the end, just judgement was delivered, and all parties involved shared a drink.[27] Again, among the Oromo people of East Africa, there existed the *Gada* system that ideally bound all. Institutions were set up to prevent violent conflict, and where violence broke out, it was checked from being escalated. Conflicts were resolved through establishing the truth, and a verdict of just and honourable peace passed. The ultimate objective being the reconciliation of parties and restoration of social harmony.[28]

Overall, effective peace-building as of necessity requires public-private sector partnerships in addressing conflicts, as in other aspects of life. This is more so, with respect to ensuring greater coordination of the numerous actors involved in the peace-building process.[29] Therefore, planning and intervention coordination of actors like international governmental organizations, bilateral donors, national governments, and international NGOs is necessary to ensure that efforts are not duplicated, and that resources are wisely utilized.

It is therefore, evident that peace-building has some linkage to development. Whether it is in the area of public, private, individual or group domain, peace-building is holistic in concept but particularistic in action. A whole array of initiatives and activities could therefore be included in the checklist of peace-building efforts. The list is substantive depending on the particular context in which it is supposed to be implemented. However, it includes or contains most of the following:[30] Election monitoring, supervision, organisation, De-mining,Disarmament, demobilisation, reintegration, Resettlement and, or repatriation of refugees and internally displaced persons, Economic assistance, construction, Legislative and judicial support, training, reform, Police and military training, Human rights monitoring, investigation, education, Institution building, Conflict resolution, mediation, and third party problem solving, Trust, confidence building, Strengthening civil society, Psychological support

With respect to the post-conflict situation in the West African sub-region we will discover that issues related to election monitoring, disarmament, demobilisation and reintegration, police and military training, institution building and the inclusion of women are key components of the various peace processes. Therefore, an examination of the efforts at peace-building in countries like Liberia, Sierra Leone and Guinea will be based on the extent to which many of the itemized requirements and other additional measures as appropriate have been met on the one hand, and the efforts made to ensure that these measures are region-friendly on the other.

Notes

1. Mohammed Mustapha Namadi, 'The Concept of Peace culture and Education for Peace-building', Paper presented at the Sub-regional Seminar on The Perspectives of Education as a Basis for Achieving a culture of Peace in Africa, Nigerian National Commission for UNESCO, August 15–17, Abuja, 2000, p.2.
2. Sara Martin, 'Concept of Peace remains elusive for many Children', *APA Monitor*, Vol.29, No.10, October.
3. Kailesh Vajpeyi, 'Paradox of Peace', 1997. Internet Site: www.lifepositive.com/mind/ethics-and-values/peace/peace-value.asp accessed in August 2004.
4. Ibid.
5. S.A. Ochoche, 'Conflict Resolution and Prevention in West Africa: The Role of Education for Tolerance and a Culture of Peace', Paper presented at the Sub-Regional Seminar on The Perspectives of Education as a Basis for Achieving a Culture of Peace in Africa, Nigerian National Commission for UNESCO, August 2000, Abuja.
6. Jacquelin Seck, *West Africa Small Arms Moratorium: High Level Consultations on the Modalities for the Implementation of PCASED*, United Nations Institute for Disarmament Research (UNIDIR), Geneva, and the United Nations Regional Centre for Peace and Disarmament in Africa (UNRCPDA), Lome, Togo, February 2000, p.6.
7. I.W Zartman (ed.), *Collapsed States: The Disintegration and Restoration of Legitimate Authority*, Boulder Co., Lynne Rienner, 1995.
8. R.A. Akindele, 'Conflict Theory, Conflict Behaviour and Conflict Control in the International System: A Theoretical Survey and Analysis', *Nigerian Journal of International Affairs*, Vol.13, No.1, 1987.
9. J.E. Dougherty and Robert Pfaltgraf Jnr., *Contending Theories of International Relations: A Comprehensive Survey*, 2nd Edn., New York, Harper and Row, 1981.

10. Tandika Nkiwane, 'The Future of Peace Keeping in Africa', *Africa Insight*, Vol.30, Nos.3-4, January 2001, p.27.
11. John Mackinlay (ed.), *A Guide to Peace Support Operations*, Providence, R.I. Brown University, Thomas J. Watson Jnr. Institute for International Studies, 1996, pp.14-15.
12. Robert Miller and Necla Tschirgi, *Canada and Missions of Peace*, Ottawa, IDRC, 2003
13. Ibid.
14. Johan Galtung, 'Cultural Violence', *Journal of Peace Research*, Vol.27, No.3, 1981, pp.291-305.
15. Boutros Boutros-Ghali, *An Agenda for Peace*, New York, United Nations, 1992, p.11.
16. Kofi Annan, *Reform Announcement*, United Nations, 16 July 1997, Part 2.
17. Chetan Kumar, *Building Peace in Haiti*, New York, International Peace Academy, Occasional Paper, 1998.
18. Gareth Evans, *Cooperating for Peace: The Global Agenda for the 1990s and Beyond*, Australia, Allen and Unwin, 1994.
19. SAIS, *The Conflict Management Toolkit: Approaches*, The Conflict Management Program, John Hopkins University. Internet Site: http://cmtoolkit.sais-jhu.edu/ accessed in August 2004.
20. Luc Reychler, 'From Conflict to Sustainable Peace-building: Concepts and Analytical Tools', Luc Reychler and Thania Paffenholz (eds.), *Peace-building: A Field Guide*, Boulder, Colorado, Lynne Rienner Publishers, 2001, p.12.
21. John Paul Lederach, *Building Peace: Sustainable Reconciliation in Divided Societies*, Washington, D.C, United States Institute of Peace, 1997, P.75.
22. Michele Maiese, *What it Means to Build a Lasting Peace*, Colorado, University of Colorado, Conflict Research Consortium, 2003.
23. SAIS, *The Conflict Management Toolkit: Approaches*, op. cit.
24. Michele Maiese, 2003, op. cit.
25. John Paul Lederach, 1997, op.cit., p.82.
26. Ibid., p.77
27. Osisioma B.C Nwolise, 'Traditional Approaches to Conflict Resolution Among the Igbo People of Nigeria: Reinforcing the Need for Africa to Rediscover its Roots', *AMANI Journal of African Peace*, Vol.1, No.1, 2004, p.61.
28. Ibid.
29. Kathleen Stephens, *Building Peace in Deeply Rooted Conflicts: Exploring New Ideas to Shape the Future*, International Understanding Conference, INCORE, 1997-01-01. Internet Site: http:www.incore.ulst.ac.uk/home/publication/conference/ciucyprus.html. Visited August 2004.
30. Robin Hay, *Peace-building During Peace Support Operations: A Survey and Analysis of Recent Missions*, Department of Foreign Affairs and International Trade, Canada, 1999, p.3.

3

An Overview of the Liberian Crisis

Background to the Crisis

Liberia is located on the West Coast of Africa, bordering the North Atlantic Ocean, and lying between Côte d'Ivoire and Sierra Leone. It has a population of about 2.8 million people and a landmass covering 97,754 sq. km (i.e. 37,743 sq. miles). It was established as an independent Republic in 1847 after its settlement by freed slaves from America in 1821. For more than a century, the country was dominated politically and economically by descendants of freed slaves otherwise referred to as 'Americo-Liberians'. In 1980, army Master Sergeant, Samuel Doe, led a bloody coup d'état in which President William Tolbert was killed. Because of a widespread dislike for the minority Americo-Liberian elite, this coup was warmly welcomed by a large segment of the Liberian population. However, it was not long before Doe increasingly became oppressive and unpopular. He surrounded himself with members of his Krahn ethnic group at the expense of others. His ruthlessness and incompetence made him feared and reviled.[1] Since the coup, rivalries between indigenous groups in search of state power became a major source of conflict and competition in Liberia. Following a coup attempt in 1985, the Armed Forces of Liberia (AFL) killed as many as 3000 Mano and Gio civilians.[2] The persecution of rival ethnic groups by the Doe regime eventually led to the efforts by the National Patriotic Force of Liberia under Charles Taylor to overthrow the Doe Regime. It was therefore, not surprising when in 1989 rebels led by Charles Taylor, a former government minister, backed by members of the Gio and Mano ethnic groups that had been subjected to severe repression, launched a guerrilla war against the Doe regime.[3] Charles Taylor prosecuted his guerrilla campaign under the

21

umbrella of the National Patriotic Front of Liberia (NPFL). Doe, who had been reported to have successfully scuttled numerous attempted coups d'état against him, about 36 coups during his rule,[4] responded to the campaign by Taylor with characteristic brutality. Even though Taylor began his putsch with less than 100 men, the NPFL soon swelled to thousands of eager but largely ill-trained volunteers. Though the campaign was initially dismissed with a wave of the hand by many, in the end Taylor and Prince Johnson, who led a splinter group of the NPFL, known as the Independent National Patriotic Front of Liberia (INPFL) overran the whole of Liberia and entered Monrovia.[5] As the war raged and the stalemate situation deepened, the immense suffering and waste of Liberian lives not only threatened the security of neighbouring states, it touched the hearts of Liberian friends and neighbours, notably Nigeria. This is however, not to say that Nigeria did not also have her interest in mind before getting involved in the Liberian crisis. Nonetheless, it is possible on the average to argue that the Nigerian involvement was largely altruistic.

Nigeria therefore, initiated and gave leadership to the formation of the ECOWAS Cease-fire Monitoring Group, otherwise known as ECOMOG. Several reasons have been adduced for the initial support given Doe by the Nigerian President. It could be argued however, that the humanitarian imperative and concerns about the war's destabilising effects on their own countries as well as regional peace and security prompted several other ECOWAS member states to consider military intervention.[6] The countries that were involved in the ECOMOG peace mission (up to 1994 and beyond) included Nigeria, Ghana, Guinea and Gambia

By 1980, the raging civil war in Liberia had claimed about 5,000 lives, and turned an additional one million Liberians, almost half of the country's population into refugees,[7] in addition of course, to thousands of internally displaced persons. The situation was bad enough to attract some level of sympathy from many African countries, though it was only a few like Nigeria and Ghana that seriously concretised this sympathy by significantly committing men and materials; and others like Mali, Gambia, Guinea and Senegal to a lesser extent.

The Standing Mediation Committee (SMC), comprising Nigeria, Ghana, Gambia, Togo and Mali after observing the carnage going on in Liberia mandated ECOMOG to: (i) seal off the 'exploding military situation until the basis of a more durable settlement could be established' and (ii) put in place a 'national conference of all Liberian political parties', (which would then choose interim administrators to run the country for about a year, preparatory to a general and presidential elections, in which Doe, Taylor, and Johnson may contest. Of course, events later overtook this).

Nigeria, under the aegis of the ECOMOG, subsequently led the ECOMOG intervention force, which later established an interim government, and purportedly blocked Taylor's path to victory twice against the government's Armed Forces of Liberia (AFL). However, by 1991, fighting had ravaged Monrovia, and President Doe was captured under very strange circumstances by the INPFL under Johnson, and subsequently tortured to death.

As a caveat, the dynamics of the Liberian civil war cannot be discussed without discussing what one may refer to as the political economy of the war. Indeed, in Africa, there is an increasingly popular view that this is the most important factor responsible for the prolongation of civil wars. For the Liberian case, the control and exploitation of diamonds, timber and other raw materials became one of the principal objectives of the warring factions. Effective control over these resources helped to finance the various factions involved in the war and gave them the means to sustain the conflict. As the war raged, it was evident that many of the protagonists had a strong financial interest in seeing the conflict prolonged. Let us also remember that the same could be said of the Angolan war, where protracted difficulties in the peace process owed much to the importance of who had control over the exploitation of the country's lucrative diamond fields. In Sierra Leone, the chance to plunder natural resources and loot the Central Bank reserves was a key motivation for those who seized power from the elected government in May 1997.[8] Also, in Central Africa, conflicts had been caused and sustained by the competition for scarce land, water resources and minerals in countries like Burundi, Rwanda, and the Democratic Republic of Congo (DRC).

In terms of multilateral response, part of the attempt by the United Nations at resolving the Liberian conflict was the establishment of the United Nations Observer Mission in Liberia (UNOMIL) in September 1993 through the UN resolution 866 to assist ECOMOG implement the Cotonou Peace Agreement.[9] It had a mandate that concentrated on the review of the disarmament and demobilization process of the factions following the peace agreements. Prior to this and even after, the following attempts, were made towards resolving the conflict

- ECOWAS Peace Plan – Banjul Communiqué (7 August 1990);
- Bamako Cease-fire (28 November 1990);
- Banjul Joint Declaration (21 December 1990);
- Lome Agreement (13 February 1991);
- Yamoussoukro I Accord (30 June 1991);
- Yamoussoukro II Accord (29 July 1991);
- Yamoussoukro III Accord (17 September 1991);

- Yamoussoukro IV Accord (30 October 1991) - UN Security Council:

Supplement to the Abuja Accord (17 August 1996).

In addition to the multilateral efforts at enhancing the peace process in Liberia, the United States on 30 September, 1993 allocated $19.83 million ($13 million of this in Economic Support Funds and the rest in Foreign Military Financing) to the UN Trust Fund for Peacekeeping in Liberia. On 20 December 1993, the US allocated an additional $11 million in support of the U.N-monitored African peacekeeping operation Liberia.[10] Also, a special conference had been convened at the ministerial level, which brought together the ECOWAS donor countries, the Bretton Woods Institutions and other relevant organs of the United Nations system. The objectives were to mobilise international political support for the peace process, help to harmonize the views of the key external political actors; and ensure that the essential resource requirements for the peace process were understood and provided for. The utility of the special conference during the peace process later prompted suggestions that this mechanism be retained to deal with the challenges of post-conflict peace-building and reconstruction.

With respect to UNOMIL as a Peace Support Operation (PSO), it contained both military and civilian components, the latter of which included political, humanitarian, and electoral personnel. Established originally for a period of seven months, UNOMIL was to comprise military observers as well as medical, engineering, communications, transportation and electoral components. It was generally mandated to:

- observe and verify both presidential and legislative elections;
- assist in the cantonment, disarmament, and demobilization of combatants;
- assist in the coordination of humanitarian assistance activities in conjunction with existing UN humanitarian relief operations;
- report on violations of humanitarian law; and
- train ECOMOG engineers in mine clearance.[11]

In 1995, UNOMIL's mandate was modified by Security Council Resolution 1020 to include investigation and reporting on violations of human rights. It was also tasked with assisting local human rights groups, as appropriate, in raising voluntary contributions for training and logistic support. There were a number of striking peace-building elements in the UNOMIL operation, which included the disarmament, demobilization and reintegration (DDR) aspects. This was absolutely necessary, for Liberia had about 50,000 to 60,000 soldiers under arms, of whom as many as 25 percent were children. It is fairly common knowledge that DDR is central to the peace-building project, given that over time, war imposes a social and economic order all of its own. As Berdal[12] pointed out, successful DDR invariably, depends on ensuring that those who benefited from this social order (warring parties and their soldiers) accept that their physical and economic security will not be adversely affected by 'relinquishing arms and abandoning what for many is not just a profession, but also a way of life'.

In the UNOMIL operation, civilians played a key role in the DDR process. The United Nations Office for the Coordination of Humanitarian Affairs (OCHA) set up a Demobilisation and Reintegration Unit responsible for co-ordinating and managing the provision of food, health services, shelter, water and sanitation for the demobilization centres amongst others. Finally, UNOMIL assisted ECOWAS in developing an electoral framework and holding elections. A UN technical survey team was dispatched in December 1996 to identify what steps would be needed to create a viable and credible framework for free and fair elections.[13] Elections were held in July 1997 with UNOMIL's Electoral Division supporting the efforts of ECOWAS, who organized and conducted the elections. Charles Taylor's NPFL and their party, which was in control of over 90 percent of the Liberian land mass won the elections and subsequently formed the government. The question which then arose was, how could the new government grapple with the serious issue of DDR and reconstruction of Liberia?

Indeed, fairly recent events indicate that though the civil war is ended, issues pertaining to reconstruction and reconciliation are still very much on the agenda. As at late September 2001, about 3,840 stranded Liberian refugees arrived Kailahun while fighting still raged in Lofa county, northwestern Liberia, with rebels committing grave human rights atrocities against civilians. Also by, early 2002, rebels of Liberians United for Reconciliation and Democracy (LURD) had advanced to a few kilometres to Monrovia, indicating that the reconciliation process in Liberia was either non-existent or had broken down at this time. ECOWAS response was to place a travel ban on LURD leadership through its Mediation and Security Committee after its Eighth Ministerial meeting held in Dakar, Senegal. ECOWAS Executive Security, Ibn Chambas, was to comment later that the ban was justified considering that the activities of the rebels ran counter to the protocols on good governance stipulated by ECOWAS and the OAU (now AU). LURD refused to attend the reconciliation preparatory meeting held 15 – 16 March 2002 at Abuja, Nigeria, citing logistical reasons. Indeed, a clear evidence that all was not well with the Liberian leadership, was the fact that Liberia had been under UN sanctions since 7 May 2001. The UN believed then that there was overwhelming evidence of the Taylor government's support for RUF rebels in Sierra Leone. The sanctions included a ban on diamond exports, an arms embargo, and travel restrictions on Liberian government officials.

In fact, to say that the resurgence of armed conflict in Liberia could be attributed to the failure of reconstruction and reconciliation process will be putting it mildly. The situation clearly lended credence to the concerns of many, that there should be both short-term and long-term strategies for bringing about reconciliation and peace in Liberia through conscious peace-building efforts.

Post-War Reconstruction and Reconciliation in Liberia

The path to ending the Liberian civil war involved the signing of over 14 Agreements while the war raged between 1990 and 1996. With the July 1997 elections, Taylor and the National Patriotic Party who won over 75 percent of the votes cast started to grapple with how to contain the very high degree of citizen dissatisfaction with governance. As earlier noted, armed insurgency and banditry still continued in some parts of Liberia with the added problem of a glaring lack of discipline among the security forces.

The war's fourteenth and final peace accord brokered in May 1996 provided for the demobilization of more than 20,000 fighters from nine rival ethnic militias under the supervision of Nigeria and other West African peacekeepers, approximately 12,000 of whom still remained in Liberia. Apart from matters of demobilization, peace-building measures for Liberia included the restructuring of the Liberian armed forces, the bureaucracy, infrastructure and utilities. Regarded as a partial success until very recently,[14] it appeared that the government was yet to meet the minimum demands of many Liberians. A Liberian peace seemed to demand every element of the peace-building repertoire, from disarmament, democratization and reintegration (DDR), through de-mining and dealing with child soldiers to human rights monitoring and elections. On the matter of disarmament, as at January 1997, about 20,000 had been disarmed.[15]

Generally, the slow pace of disarmament was attributed in part to suspicions among the faction leaders, a lack of incentives offered to belligerents to disarm, and inaccurate figures on combatants. The disarmament statistics as at 31 January 1997, showed that 20,362 soldiers were disarmed out of a total of 32,200 estimated force. Of these, 11,553 were from the NPFL out of an estimated force of 12,500, 571 were from the AFL of an estimated force of 7,000, 5622 were from ULIMO of an estimated force of 6,800; while 2,616 others disarmed came from other smaller groups.[16] As at 1999, about 31,000 weapons had been surrendered by ex-combatants, and included handguns and assault rifles.[17] ECOMOG participated actively in this disarmament exercise. Indeed, the destruction of weapons of war ceremony in Liberia formally marked the end of the peacekeeping mission in the country.

It is understandable that the issue of disarmament should be topmost on the agenda for bringing about peace and stability in Liberia. Indeed, the problem posed by 'floating weapons', especially light weapons has in recent times been of grave concern to leaders of the member states of ECOWAS. For instance, it was estimated that at a point in time, about 15 million weapons were in circulation in the sub-region, working out at about one weapon to 25 persons. It was against this background and the experiences of the successful DDR in Mali after their civil war that ECOWAS Heads of State on 31st October 1998 adopted a Moratorium on the importation, exportation and manufacture of light weapons and its availability in West Africa. For peace to reign in Africa, and for wars to be avoided, this issue of light weapons needs to be more seriously addressed.

Another problem arising from the Liberian civil war was the issue of child soldiers and what to do about the unacceptable development. Children who had been used as child soldiers were amongst the most tragic victims of this war. Although, international law forbids the use of children under the age of fifteen as soldiers, thousands of such children were used in the Liberian civil war. Many were killed during this conflict and denied the most basic right – the right to life. Yet, others were deprived of their liberty – forcibly conscripted by warring factions and separated from their families against their wills, some were forced to kill or torture others with the consequent severe psychological trauma. No doubt, all had been denied a normal childhood. Of the estimated 60,000 fighters involved in the conflict, UNICEF estimated that 6,000 of the fighters, or 10 percent, were children under fifteen.[18] Further, some estimate that another 20 percent of the fighters were between the ages of fifteen and seventeen.

Experience so far, shows that the reintegration of these children back into their communities is a herculean task. More often than not, their parents had been killed, and in some cases their families separated, with no relations to run to. In others, families refused to take the children back because of the abuses they had committed against humanity. A Liberian civil organization, the Children's Assistance Programme (CAP) was in the forefront in trying to rehabilitate and reintegrate the child soldiers. Also there were community-based transit homes run by UNICEF which also assisted in this rehabilitation.

With respect to the Liberian civil society since the end of war in 1997, what we have is a situation in which the government exercised a preponderant amount of state power, thereby suffocating the civil society. For instance, there were only a few radio stations in Liberia, prominent amongst which included Charles Taylor's Kiss-FM, the only country wide FM Station. Others included the radio station managed by the Roman Catholic Church, and the Swiss Hirondelle Foundation's Star Radio, which broadcasts civic education programming. However, it is interesting to note that a highly restrictive media law enacted under the Doe regime gave the Ministry of Information in Liberia broad powers to control the media. The control over the media served to constrain the social and political spaces left for civil society to operate and contribute to the peace-building process.

There are however, a number of civil society groups, including human rights organizations that operate in Monrovia and environs and that have enhanced the reconciliation process. One of these is the Catholic Peace and Justice Commission. In the Liberian post-civil war situation, the manner women have been treated appear to vary according to cultural practices, religion and social status. However, many women continue to suffer from physical abuse and traditional societal discrimination despite constitutionally guaranteed equality. Several women's organizations assisted the estimated 25,000 women who had been raped and abused during the war.[19]

In terms of the political situation in the country after the war, Charles Taylor and the National Patriotic Party were continually accused of high-handedness and intransigence. His government was accused by other segments of the Liberian political spectrum of not implementing aspects of the peace process. For example, that relating to the reorganisation of the military. Also, sporadic attacks on mosques in several parts of the country raised tension among the Mandingo Muslims and other groups in the country.

Liberia's economy was largely burdened by its $3 billion debt. Arrears on loan repayments disqualifed the country from IMF assistance and detered private lending. Corruption is still a major obstacle to economic growth, and much of the output of Liberia's diamond mines continue to be smuggled untaxed from the country.

Ironically, the saddening news of renewed rebel activities in Liberia in 2002 questioned the whole array of efforts at reconstruction and reconciliation.[19] The armed incursions appeared to have originated from the disenchantment of some fighters, purportedly recruited in Sierra Leone, who claimed to have been marginalized by the Lome Peace process. The point remains however, that the necessity for peace and peace-building measures in Liberia and the sub-region as a whole remain a paramount matter. For Liberia, the following issues will continue to attract peace-building initiatives, namely: disarmament and rehabilitation of former fighters, therapy and counselling, caring for child victims of the war, repatriation and resettlement of refugees and displaced persons, promoting national unity and minimizing ethnic differences. Observing the Liberian situation, it is possible to predict that half-hearted attempts or outright refusal to re-integrate estranged Liberians into the body politic could result into a resurgence of the conflict, with dire consequences for the peace process and the Liberian citizenry.

However, a positive development, which energized the reconciliation and reconstruction process of the war-torn country, was the sudden exit of Charles Taylor from Liberia.[20] In August of 2003, he was persuaded to abdicate his Presidency, and he left Liberia for a new home in Calabar, South-eastern Nigeria, on political exile. This was as a result of the compressive peace Agreement (CPA) after signed on 18 August 2003 by rebel leaders, politicians and government officials under the supervision of ECOWAS. The Agreement called for a two-year power sharing arrangement that will lead to new elections in Liberia, and which excluded top rebel leaders from the government. Taylor's exit and his acceptance by Nigeria raised a lot of concern. Those who wanted Taylor tried for war crimes and crime against humanity could not just understand why he should be allowed to escape to Nigeria. On the other hand, ECOWAS Heads of States and the Nigerian government explained that since Charles Taylor was seen as constituting the problem rather than a solution to the Liberian crisis, it was imperative to diplomatically remove him from the scene. This was necessary if peace was to have a chance in Liberia. Though, it was not easy to convince all, some countries like the United States, later saw the wisdom in this line of action taken by the ECOWAS leaders. Oftentimes, these leaders had always called for African solutions to African conflicts. This was an opportunity to see how this works in practice. So far, this appears to have been a right diplomatic intervention. Again, Nigeria's diplomacy and leverage was instrumental in reaching this Agreement. Even when there were calls for Charles Taylor to be handed over to be tried by a War Crimes Tribunal, Nigeria remained adamant and faithful to the terms of Agreement under which Charles Taylor accepted to leave Liberia on political exile. The lesson to be learned from this is that this option of offering political asylum or of 'diplomatically removing key actors and their families from the theatre of war' should be included amongst the repertoire of peace building measures in Africa. Though, this may not sometimes be morally defensible, it is however, germane to achieving immediate cessation of conflict and stopping the loss of lives, and may invariably enhance the peace process.

The immediate imperative for building peace in post-conflict Liberia after Charles Taylor entails ensuring security in all parts of the country, especially in those areas where the government still does not have complete control. Though the partnership between the Transitional Government and the United Nations is functional, what is important in the long-term, is really is for Liberians to be able to manage their own affairs. It is therefore important that the international community and ECOWAS continue to support the reconstruction and peace-building measures already on the ground. However, the reconstruction and reconciliation efforts in Sierra Leone and Guinea may amount to nothing if Liberia is not at peace. Therefore, a regional peace-building framework as a strategy of ensuring stability is imperative.

There has been what one may consider a monumental development in the political environment in Liberia after the exit of Charles Taylor with the successful elections held on 11 October 2005 that saw Ellen Johnson Sirleaf as Liberia's, and indeed, Africa's first elected female President. Eventhough the Presidential election went through a run-off exercise, it was overall declared free and fair by most observers both local and international. The success of this post-transition election in Liberia in a way justified the efforts at peacebuilding in the country made by Nigeria, ECOWAS, the United Nations mission in Liberia (UNMIL), the civil society and the international community, who all pulled resources together to promote peace education and peacebuilding in Liberia.

Notes

1. Eric G. Berman and Katie E. Sams, *Peacekeeping in Africa: Capabilities and Culpabilities*, Geneva, UNIDIR, 2000, p.83.
2. Herbert Howe, 'Lessons of Liberia: ECOMOG and Regional Peacekeeping', in E. Michael et al. (eds.), *Nationalism and Ethnic Conflict*, Cambridge, The MIT Press, 1997.3. Freedom in the World 1998–1999. Http.//www.freedomhouse.org/survey/country/liberia. Visited October 2001.
4. Solomon O. Ogwu, 'Nigeria and the Liberian Imbroglio: An Epitome of Nigeria-led Crisis Resolution in the Sub-Region', *Nigerian Forum*, Vol.13, Nos.9-10, September-October, 1994.
5. Lynda Schuster, 'The Final Days of Dr. Doe', *Granta*, No.48, summer 1994, p.66.
6. Eric G. Berman and Katie E. Sams, 2000, op cit., p.84.
7. Celestine Bassey, 'Nigeria and Regional Security in the West African Sub-Region: Lessons from Monrovia', *Nigerian Forum,* January-February, Vol.14, Nos.1-2, 1994, p.35.
8. United Nations, *The Causes of Conflict and the Promotion of Durable Peace and Sustainable Development in Africa,* Report of the Secretary-General to the United Nations Security Council, 16 April, 1998.
9. Robin Hay, *Peace-building During Peace Support Operations: A Survey and Analysis of Recent Missions,* Canada, Department of Foreign Affairs of International Trade, March 14, 1999, p.7.
10. Human Rights Watch/Africa, *Easy Prey: Child Soldiers in Liberia*, 1994, p.53.

11. United Nations, 16 April 1998, op cit, p.6.
12. Mats R. Berdal, 'Disarmament and Demobilization After Civil Wars: Arms, Soldiers and the Termination of Armed Conflicts', London International Institute for Strategic Studies, *Adelphi paper 303*, 1996, p.73.
13. Robin Hay, 1999, op cit, p.8.
14. Matthew Mbu, 'A Reappraisal of Nigeria's Foreign Policy', *Emwai Centre for Political and Economic Research Journal*, Vol.5, No.2, 1997, pp.92 - 101.
15. Basic Papers, *Africa: The Challenge of Light Weapons Destruction during Peacekeeping Operations*, Basic Publications, No.23, December 1997, p.14.
16. Ibid. In Conjunction with voluntary disarmament, ECOMOG troops actively sought out arms caches. In December 1996, ECOMOG forces recovered a large cache of arms including assault rifles and pistols. A cache seized at the residence of Alhaji Koromah, leader of ULIMO-K, and a candidate in the Presidential elections included an anti-aircraft gun, two mortars, 600 bombs, 80 grenades, 86 rifles and 40,613 rounds of ammunition.
17. The West African Bulletin, 'Farewell to Arms in Liberia', No.7, October, 1999.
18. *Human Rights Watch/Africa*, 1994, p.2.
19. Osita Agbu, 'Sub-regional Dynamics of the Resurgent Conflicts in Liberia', *Nigerian Forum*, Vol.23. Nos. 9-10, 2002. p.275.
20. Tewroh-Wehtoe, 'Taylor's Exit Spells Hope for a Troubled Nation', *The Liberian Dialogue*, Sungbeh Communications. See Internet Site- http://theliberiandialogue.org/articles/. Accessed August 2004.

4

An Overview of the Sierra Leonean Crisis

Background to the Crisis

Sierra Leone is located on the South West Coast of Africa sandwiched between Guinea and Liberia. It has a landmass of 71,740 sq. km (i.e. 27,699 sq. miles), and has a population of about 5.2 million people, with capital at Freetown.[1] It gained political independence from the United Kingdom on 27 April 1961. Beginning from 1991, Sierra Leone was embroiled in a brutal civil war, which witnessed the rebel movement, the Revolutionary United Front (RUF), fighting against three successive governments. In other words, this is a country that had been subjected to 10 years of continuous civil war with the resultant human and material destruction usually associated with such wars. In this war, the civilian populace bore the brunt of man's bestiality to man.

In terms of its economy, the country has since independence depended on the export of agricultural produce, minerals and marine resources. Principal among which include coffee, cocoa, palm kernels and palm oil. Of the mineral resources, which had helped to exacerbate the civil war, diamonds had for long played a major role in the economy. At certain periods, diamonds accounted for over 70 percent of the nation's foreign exchange earnings. Gold, rutile and bauxite, have all also served as prime sources of revenue. Therefore, whether in terms of mineral resources or agricultural produce, and even marine or forest resources, Sierra Leone presents an enticing proposition for businessmen and soldiers of fortune.

In terms of its ethnic composition, this is rather varied. Fourteen main groups form the bulk of the population. In the South and Southeast are mainly the Mendes, Sherbros, Vais, Kissis and Kono. In the North, the Femnes, Limbas, Kurankos, Mandingos, Susus and Yalunkas. In the western area, with the capital Freetown, there are visible intermixes among the various groups over the

32

generations, blurring the linguistic and cultural distinctions of any one group, especially the Creoles.[2]

The All Peoples Congress (APC) dominated the political history of Sierra Leone in the years shortly after independence in 1961 and for over twenty odd years in the main. In its early days, this party comprised northerners to be joined later by the Creoles of the western area and later by the Konos of the Eastern region, in a united opposition to the ruling Sierra Leone Peoples Party (SLPP).

The civil war in Sierra Leone began when the RUF entered Eastern Sierra Leone at Bomaru in Kailahun District from Liberian territory controlled by Charles Taylor on 23 March 1991.[3] The RUF predominantly formed by political exiles, mainly students and intellectuals initially had the political objective of overthrowing Joseph Momoh's one-party rule and restoring multi-party democracy in the country. Some of the RUF rebels had gained warfare experience under the NPFL, and had learnt various aspects of guerrilla tactics. The RUF was subsequently encouraged and supplied logistics and materials by Charles Taylor, and also supported by Burkinabe and Liberian mercenaries for other selfish reasons. For Charles Taylor, his support was perceived as a way of getting back at Momoh's government in Sierra Leone for supporting ECOMOG, and for allowing the ULIMO faction in Liberian conflict to operate out of the bases in Sierra Leone. For him also, the destabilization of the border area with Sierra Leone ensured that they could access parts of the clandestine trade in diamond from Sierra Leone.[4]

The RUF was headed by ageing Foday Sankoh and began just like the NPFL with a small band of around 100 fighters. However, through various forms of conscription of youths, its ranks soon swelled to several hundreds, and by the summer of 1991 it was in control of a significant amount of southern and eastern Sierra Leone.

In summary, the rebels did not succeed in gaining any form of power in Sierra Leone until 1997, after six gruelling years of civil war and three military coups. President Momoh's response to the rebel insurgency was both ineffective and unpopular, especially with the Sierra Leonean Army (SLA). It was therefore not very surprising when in May 1992, a group of junior SLA officers led by a 28-year-old Valentine Strasser overthrew Momoh. Still, the rebels continued their insurgency and Strasser had to seek security assistance from Nigeria, the Kamajors (a Sierra Leonean militia) and the private security company - Executive outcomes (EO). In turn, Strasser who was not necessarily protected by EO was overthrown by his Chief of Defence Staff, Brig.General Julius Maada Bio. Bio eventually agreed to an election scheduled for February 1996, and stood down. Ahmed Tejan Kabbah of the Sierra Leone People's Party (SLPP) subsequently emerged as President. Though he had democratic legitimacy, Kabbah had very little political and economic power, and fell to another military coup led by Major Paul Koroma and the Armed Forces Ruling Council (AFRC) on 25 May 1997. At this stage, Sankoh instructed the RUF to support the AFRC, and an unholy alliance was formed between the two, with RUF members appointed to senior positions in the new government. Sankoh who was under house arrest, was nevertheless, named as Koroma's deputy.[5] This development was to lead to the intervention of external actors in the Sierra Leonean civil war.

Nigeria intervened through ECOMOG to try and unseat the Johnny Koroma junta. Sierra Leone had a bilateral defence agreement with Nigeria signed in March 1997, which allowed for the training of Sierra Leone's army and the presidential guard. Smaller contingents from Ghana and Guinea were subsequently called upon to assist the Nigerian troops numbering around 3,500 in Sierra Leone. However, soon the ECOMOG campaign in Sierra Leone ran into a deadlock as even though it controlled Lungi Airport outside Freetown; the AFRC controlled Freetown, the capital, and some of the other major cities, whereas large tracts of the hinterland were virtually in nobody's control.[6]

Efforts aimed at resolving the conflict diplomatically resulted in a peace accord, signed in Conakry, Guinea on 23 October 1997. However, this effort collapsed due mainly to the AFRC and Johnny Paul Koroma's lack of faith in the document and their lack of transparency in resolving the conflict. However, in a dramatic move, the months of diplomatic quagmire were swept away in less than a week of fighting when ECOMOG stormed Freetown and 'liberated' the capital from the clutches of the combined forces of rebellious soldiers and the RUF. Tejan Kabbah's SLPP government was reinstated, though ECOMOG was still unable to control the hinterland, just as was the experience during the Liberian civil war. The RUF and their allies, the rebellious SLA soldiers returned to the bush and wreaked havoc in the countryside, killing, looting, maiming and raping in the process. There were large-scale human rights abuses by the rebels variously categorized by them as 'operation pay yourself', 'operation no living-thing', and 'Rebel roulette'. The first two are self-explanatory, but the third categorization, 'Rebel roulette' demands some clarification. According to Boas,[7] this is akin to a deadly game by the rebels in which those captured are forced to draw pieces of paper from a hat or bowl in order to decide what limb or human part should be removed from their body like ear, nose, finger, hand, leg etc. This is indeed cruelty beyond imagination and goes to indicate why the reconciliation process in Sierra Leone is a very difficult one.

It is however, to the credit of the Kamajors that they assisted the Kabbah government, and generally maintained security in the Mende-dominated areas in parts of southeastern Sierra Leone. Though, also accused of human rights violations and the scramble for diamonds just like some ECOMOG soldiers, they are perceived to have played a positive role when the story of the civil war in Sierra Leone is told.

It was the RUF's fairly successful counter-attack in January 1999, when they broke through ECOMOG defences to enter Freetown for a few days, that convinced many that it was time to pursue more vigorously a diplomatic end to this conflict. At this period, Nigeria, the key player in the region and in ECOMOG, was undergoing a political transition that will see to the end of military rule and the enthronement of democracy in the potentially strong but embattled country. The civil society in Nigeria was increasingly complaining of the cost of the peace mission in Sierra Leone, while also smarting from the inability of the federal government to adequately provide basic social services. In short, the message from the emerging democratic leadership in Nigeria was therefore, that the country was no longer able to bear the political and economic costs of its military involvement in Sierra Leone. This outcry which got the listening ear of the international community probably led to more intensified efforts at brokering peace, and ultimately to the peace agreement between the RUF and the Kabbah government, signed in Lome, Togo, in July 1999.

Though there have been a few incidents since the agreement was signed, such as the temporary capture and release of 500 UN troops in May 2000, and the arrest and detention of Foday Sankoh after a shooting incident outside his house, generally, the ceasefire subsequently brokered by ECOWAS in 2000 prevented a relapse into renewed violence or war. There was also the large presence of UN forces and British troops, which helped to deter would-be trouble-shooters from attempting renewed conflict. Sierra Leone appears calm now, and may be able to sustain the peace achieved if the conflicts in the neighbouring countries like Liberia and Guinea do not upset the delicate balance. Again, the situation indicates the necessity for approaching the conflicts in this part of Africa from a regional perspective rather than seeking only a country-by-country solution. This are not to say that country level analysis and prescriptions is not important, but ultimately, to achieve sustainable peace requires a regional approach.

The Sierra Leonean civil war on the whole, revealed that the traditional structure of antagonism was complex. Again, it appeared that the use of violence as a means of achieving political and economic power is deeply rooted in the Sierra Leonean political culture.[8] In addition, the role-played by external actors driven purely by economic interests helped to deepen and extend the war. For example, Liberia, Burkina Faso, and Libya supported the RUF and AFRC, through providing arms and logistics. There were mercenaries from the UK, South Africa, Ukraine and other Eastern European countries. While EO, a Southern Africa-based security firm was contracted by the Sierra Leonean government in 1995, elements from Ukraine and other East European countries fought on the side of the RUF.[9] In fact, Zack-Williams,[10] was to argue that the Sierra Leonean conflict had hardly any ethnic or religious dimension, usually common to many other civil wars. This is disputable. However, the economic factor as an explanation appeared more realistic as the war progressed. This is not to say that some colonial policies did not favour some ethnic groups which later resulted in perceived marginalization by the others. For instance, it was pointed out that the Mende were favoured by colonial policies,[11] though the war in Sierra Leone arose directly from the social inequalities prevailing in the country.

Post-War Reconstruction and Reconciliation in Sierra Leone

The duration of the civil war in Sierra Leone and the brutality, which characterized this war made matters of reconstruction and reconciliation extremely important, especially considering that relative stability was subsequently achieved. The international community tried at different stages of the conflict to assist in the reconstruction process. For instance, the UN presence in Sierra Leone expanded significantly from February 1998, and by July 1998, the UN Security Council approved a measure to establish the UN observer mission to Sierra Leone (UNOMSIL). Again, the UN provided significant support for the setting up of the Truth and Reconciliation commission, and the National Human Rights Commission according to the Lome peace agreement, in addition to assisting in the registration of ex-combatants.[12]

UNOMSIL, initially established for six months by resolution 1181 was to promote stability and security by disarming and demobilizing former combatants. Security Council resolution 1181 was particularly concerned with the plight of civilians in the conflict. It expressed concern over the immense suffering and deaths that the conflict had visited upon refugees and displaced persons, especially children. It condemned the continuing violence against civilians carried out by the ousted junta of Johnny Koroma and called for a process of national reconciliation to finally end the war. Indeed, the resolution offered a precedent for including children's needs in future post conflict peace-building PSOs.[13] Further, the military observers, initially 40 in number, were to monitor the disarmament and demobilization of former combatants and the role of ECOMOG in providing security and in the collection and destruction of arms in secure areas. The civilian component of the operation involved advising the government and police officials on police practice, training, re-equipment and recruitment.[14] In particular, on the need to respect internationally accepted standards of policing in democratic societies. It involved basically, advice on the police reform and restructuring in Sierra Leone. On the whole, resolution 1181 encouraged the international community to assist and participate in the longer-term task of reconstruction, economic and social recovery and development in Sierra Leone. In addition, it also encouraged the Sierra Leone government to co-ordinate an effective national response to the needs of children, especially child soldiers generated by the conflict.

Mention should be made of the kinds of external assistance received during and immediately after this war. Indeed, there is no gainsaying that this helped in firming up the peace process in Sierra Leone. From May 1998, the United Kingdom (UK), the European Union (EU) and United States (US) issued several statements denouncing human rights violations committed by the AFRC/RUF in Sierra Leone. The EU and US also offered logistic and financial support to ECOMOG and humanitarian relief to thousands of refugees and displaced persons. By 1999, western countries partly in response to Nigeria's threat to withdraw from Sierra Leone in view of the then emerging civilian dispensation in the country stepped up their support for ECOMOG. The UK pledged an additional US $1.65 million matching grant. As at mid-1999, US $7 million of those sums had been used to ensure logistical support to ECOMOG.[15] However, while some of these countries were commended for their assistance, France was specifically accused of having supplied weapons to the RUF through Burkina Faso and Liberia.[16] As part of the peace-building efforts in Sierra Leone, the World Bank in 2002, agreed in principle to allocate over US $140 million to support reconstruction and development efforts and fight against HIV/AID in Sierra Leone.[17]

More importantly, we should note that no complete discussion of the peace-building efforts in Sierra Leone would be complete without x-raying the Lome Peace Accord of 7 July 1999 between the Government of Sierra Leone and the RUF. The issues under this accord related to political, military, humanitarian, human rights and socio-economic matters. A major aspect which laid the foundation for this Accord was the recognition that a military 'solution' cannot in itself address the causes of the Sierra Leonean war. And that peace-making efforts should instead be directed toward fostering broad-based, inclusive processes capable of addressing the underlying causes of war, with support for economic regeneration to encourage the voluntary demobilization of armed combatants.[18]

Let us also observe that from the outbreak of the war in 1991, there were three attempts to bring the conflict to an end through a negotiated settlement: the Abidjan Peace Agreement in November 1996, the Conakry Peace Plan in October 1997, and of course, the Lome Peace Agreement in July 1999. In these negotiations, the terms of agreement primarily centred on the principle of power-sharing and amnesty and the role of foreign troops but also included provisions for social and economic rehabilitation and reintegration.[19] With the outbreak of fighting in Sierra Leone in May 2000, the implementation of the 1999 Lome Agreement was severally compromised; nevertheless, many Sierra Leoneans continued to affirm the importance of this Agreement and the need to apply it in the current peace-building efforts.

Disarmament, Democratisation and Reintegration in the Peace Process

One of the major success stories of the peace process in Sierra Leone is the DDR programme. This lasted from September 1998 to the year 2002. The DDR programme committed the Tejan Kabbah government to the complete disarmament, demobilisation and re-integration of an estimated 45,000 combatants.[20] Suffice it to say that the success of any peace-building in post-conflict societies depends a great deal on the ability to remove excess and illicit weapons from the system. It also involves the immediate stabilization and management of what has been considered legitimate stockpiles.

For Sierra Leone, the disarmament process was conceived as part of a comprehensive framework for DDR. While the DDR programme was conducted under the policy direction of the National Committee on Disarmament, Demobilisation and Re-integration (NCDDR), the disarmament was carried out practically by ECOMOG and the United Nations Mission in Sierra Leone (UNOMSIL). On the whole, a total of 42,300 weapons and about 1.2 million pieces of ammunition were collected and destroyed, while 72,490 combatants from the various fighting groups were disarmed and demobilized.[21]

Tables 1, 2 and 3 show the total number of combatants disarmed by groups, total number of weapons and ammunition collected in all districts, and the types of weapons collected during the disarmament process.A National Committee for Disarmament, Demobilization and Reintegration (NCDDR) was established by the SLPP government charged with the responsibility of consolidating the existing short-term security in the country. The tables are largely self-explanatory, but all point to significant success in the disarmament process.

Table 1: Total disarmed by group

Category Disarmament	PHASE I (Sept-Dec 1998)	PHASE II (Oct.1999-2000)	Interim Phase (May 2000 – May 2001)	PHASE III (May 2001 – Jan.2002)	Total
RUF	187	4,130	768	19,267	24,352
AFRC	0	2,129	445	0	2,574
Discharged/ Ex SA	2,994	2,366	593	0	5,953
CDF	2	8,800	524	28,051	37,377
Other (including Paramilitary)	0	1,473	298	463	2,234
Total	**3,183**	**18,898**	**2,628**	**47,781**	**72,490**

Source: NCDDR, August 2002

Table 2: Weapons and Ammunition Collected in all districts

Type	Total
Hand Weapons	7,785
Assault Weapons	17,180
Group Weapons	1,036
Ammunition	935,495

Source: NCDR, August 2002

Table 3: Types of Weapons Collected

Weapons	Types
Assorted (ex-Kabala)	135
Ak-47	4,224
Ak-58	1,061
FN Rifle	413
SAR	447
G-III	924
LMG	140
RPG-7	217
Mortar	45
Others	2,742
Hand Grenade	1,856
Pistols	493
Pre 4 NOV 1999	141
Assorted (discharged SLA)	1,969
Total	**14,807**

Source: M and E Unit, ES-NCDDR, UNAMSIL and ECOMOG, May 2000.

The NCDDR itself was set up by the Sierra Leonean government with the help of the international community. It basically brought together all the stakeholders in the peace process, including leaders of the various warring factions, the peacekeeping forces and donor representatives, with the Sierra Leone Head of State as the chairman. The following are the stated goals of the DDR programme:

(a) Collect, register, destroy and dispose all conventional weapons and ammunition retrieved from combatants during the disarmament process.

(b) Demobilise approximately 45,000 combatants comprising the following factions: The Armed forces of Sierra Leone (SLA) – 6,000; Armed Forces Revolutionary Council (AFRC); Revolutionary United Front (RUF) – 15,000, Civil Defence Force – 15,000 and Paramilitary forces as designated in the Lome Agreement 2000.

(c) Prepare for the sustainable social and economic reintegration of all ex-combatants for long-term security.[21]

Generally, the disarmament and demobilization process ran over three main phases, with an interim phase added in 2000. The phases are as follows:

a) Phase I: September – December 1998
b) Phase II: October 1999 – April 2000
c) Interim Phase: May 2000 – May 2001
d) Phase III: May 2000 – January 2002.

Statistics from Table 1 show that Phase III of the programme was clearly the most successful. It was under this phase that 43,509 out of the 62,618 adult soldiers were disarmed. This phase also resulted in the disarming of 4,272 out of an estimated 6,845 child soldiers. In short, under this phase, 68.79 per cent or about 7 out of every 10 ex-combatants were disarmed. The degree of success of this disarmament programme led to the symbolic burning of about 3,000 weapons on 18 January 2002 at Lungi Town, in a ceremony that marked the end of the war in Sierra Leone. A community Arms collection and Destruction (CA&D) programme, which yielded a total of 1,036 shortguns and a few other weapons ensured that the programme was conclusive in its implementation.

Civil Society and the Peace Process

Though recognised as important in creating an enabling environment that will make peace possible, it was evident that the civil society in Sierra Leone was virtually excluded from the peace process. Though the National Commission for Democracy and Human Rights did hold a three-day consultative Conference of parliamentarians, paramount chiefs, political parties and other civic organizations in April 1999, this was considered an insignificant contribution. It largely endorsed the legitimacy of the Kabbah government and the Abidjan and Conakry Agreements as the basis for negotiated settlement, but strongly objected to any form of power sharing with the RUF-AFRC. Despite this position taken by the consultative conference, the Lome Agreement included provisions for power sharing, partly due to pressure from the Presidents of Burkina Faso, Liberia, Nigeria and Togo. Nevertheless, there was little direct participation of Sierra Leonean civil society organizations in the Abidjan process and limited involvement at Lome. For the Lome Agreement, the role of the Inter-Religious council was unique. It was instrumental in initiating dialogue with the RUF and Charles Taylor of Liberia, and has continued to play a supporting role in the implementation of the Agreement.[23]

However, a diverse cast of civil society groups and individuals were very active in mobilizing public opinion in favour of peace and democratisation, with some operating from abroad. A return to democratic governance was the

41

main focus of many of the civil society organisations like the Mano River Bridge Initiative, and the National Co-ordinating Committee for peace (NCCP) which lasted only six months, and consisted of civil society groups like the Women's Movement for Peace, the Council of Churches in Sierra Leone and the Teachers' Union. The Sierra Leone Labour Congress was also one of the prime movers of NCCP. The Sierra Leone women's Movement for Peace (SLWMP) was equally active as part of the broader women's movement.[24]

Among the numerous players involved in shaping the Lome Peace Agreement, the Inter-Religious Council of Sierra Leone (IRCSL) stood out as the most visible and effective NGO bridge builder between the government, the warring factions and a devastated population. The IRCSL which represented about sixty per cent Muslims and fifteen to twenty per cent Christians of the total population in the country, mobilized churches and mosques around the country to preach against violence, and also to preach reconciliation for all. The council's main strategy was to remain neutral and supportive of the mediation process. Recognised by regional foreign ministers for having 'kick-started' the Lome Peace Process, IRCSL members became integral facilitators of the talks. The IRCSL earned the respect of civil society, the parties to the conflict and the international community. It was able to achieve this status through consultative meetings with key players, press releases, communiqués, experience sharing, and prayers through its preaching of God's message of repentance, forgiveness and reconciliation.[25]

By and large, Sierra Leone has established a unique track record for a post-conflict country. Within a year of the end of its brutal war, the country achieved a growth rate of six per cent, while inflation fell to zero per cent. Over 300,000 displaced persons and refugees have been resettled and more than 70,000 combatants disarmed and demobilized.[26] Due to this impressive post-conflict rebuilding, development partners pledged more financial and technical support for the country, with emphasis shifting from humanitarian to development assistance. Generally, successful completion of the DDR programme, long-term support in rebuilding the country's armed forces and police force, and support for the Truth and Reconciliation Commission (TRC) and Special Court were seen as essential to ensuring Sierra Leone's development. The Sierra Leonean government on its own identified, and committed itself to addressing major developmental challenges, mainly issues that have to do with inclusion, good governance, decentralization, equity and sustainable growth. It also expressed intention to focus attention on basic education and primary health care, while spurring on economic growth through private sector partnership, stimulating agriculture and reviving the mining industry amongst others.[27] The prayer at this stage is for the Government of Sierra Leone to frontally address those problems that created the objective conditions for the civil war in the first place. These conditions are still persisting. Issues that have to do with marginalization and the alienation of the youth from the country's development plan need to be urgently addressed.

Justice and Reconciliation

A very important aspect of the peace process in Sierra Leone considering the enormity of the human rights abuses during the war was the issue of Justice and Reconciliation. The Lome agreement had provided for a blanket amnesty which many felt was unacceptable, even though, there was the need to envision a process that will foster truth and reconciliation as was the case in South Africa and Rwanda. Perhaps, this was why 'The Truth and Reconciliation Commission' (TRC) was established through the Truth and Reconciliation Act of 22 February 2000. This was in line with Article XXIV of the Lome Peace Agreement. TRC was mandated by this Act to create an impartial record of violations of human rights and humanitarian law, to address impunity, to assist the victims to promote healing and reconciliation and to prevent a repetition of the abuses. The TRC was empowered to summon anyone to testify before it. The philosophical and psychological foundation of measures like this is anchored on the basis that coming out in the open to tell the truth about what actually happened can heal the victim and liberate the perpetrators. Without the truth as hard as that may be, there may not be any reconciliation. The TRC is not necessarily a Court of Law, and appearing before it does not lead to imprisonment. It was in principle designed for everyone, victims, families, witnesses and perpetrators, while a Special Court will be set up to try those who bear the greatest responsibility for the abuses.[28] Perhaps, this was why some called for an international trial of the leader of the RUF, Foday Sankoh, for his activities against humanity during the civil war. However, determining how far the TRC could meet its objectives is difficult to say. Experience indicates that many of those guilty of perpetuating heinous crimes against humanity usually refuse to appear before Truth Commissions.

Peace-Building and the Legacy of Terror

This is an aspect of the Sierra Leonean war that merits a revisitation. The extensive use of terror during the 10-year period of the war was simply mind-boggling. This had serious implications for the success or otherwise of the rehabilitation and reconciliation process. The atrocities are better documented for posterity, as it holds great lessons for nations and individuals alike.

The rebel incursion into Freetown on 6 January 1999 brought to the capital the atrocities which had been rampant in the north and east of the country after the rebel forces of the AFRC and RUF were forced from power by troops of the ECOWAS Cease-fire Monitoring Group (ECOMOG) in February 1998. Although, it is near impossible to ascertain the exact number of civilian deaths during the rebel incursion into Freetown, the UN Observer Mission in Sierra Leone (UNOMSIL) estimated up to 5,000 people, at least 2,000 of them civilians. Medical authorities in Freetown subsequently put the figure at over 6,000.[29]

Generally, rape and other forms of sexual abuse against women and girls by rebel forces were systematic and widespread. Women and girls were often rounded up and gang-raped by rebel forces. According to a witness who had been abducted by rebel forces, women and girls held captive by rebel forces were told to submit to rape or otherwise be killed.[30] Up to 200,000 people became homeless in and around Freetown, and thousands fled to neighbouring Guinea and other countries in the region. There was extensive destruction of property, particularly east of Freetown where about 90 percent of buildings were destroyed. In addition, ECOMOG forces, together with the civilian militia, which supported President Ahmed Tejan Kabbah, the Civil Defence Forces (CDF), were also accused of committing human rights violations, though on a smaller scale than the rebel forces. ECOMOG was accused of arbitrary beatings and summary executions of suspected rebels.

However, as noted earlier, members of the AFRC/RUF perpetrated the vast majority of abuses. For instance, in an interview conducted by Human Rights Watch[31] in June 1998, over 425 survivors of gunshots, amputations and other mutilations, or rape were registered in Connaught, Magburaka, and Makeni hospitals in Sierra Leone. Approximately 82 survivors of these same types of abuses were identified in Guinea at Conakry, Faranah, Kisidougou, and Gueckedou hospitals during roughly the same period.

It is common knowledge that women suffer immensely during wars.[32] Generally, women and especially girls in Sierra Leone during this period suffered gender-related problems such as sexual assault, rape and commercial sexual exploitation. The girls suffered not only the psychological trauma of unwanted pregnancies, but also the trauma that arises from being rejected by their communities. Note however, that the closest women came to participating in the war itself were as nurses and officers in the army, helping with the wounded. There were a few women on the RUF side. Some in fact, acted as officers and combatants, and played a crucial role in the way female prisoners of war were treated. They sometimes supported and advocated for the release of female prisoners.[33] Active women NGOs that supported peace-building measures included the Women's Movement for Peace (WMP), which mobilized women to broker peace between the warring parties; Women Organized for a Morally Enlightened Nation (WOMEN); and Women International League for Peace and Freedom (WILPF) Sierra Leone. Generally, women were not given the opportunity to contribute effectively to the peace process due to their low-level representation at the political level, especially during the various conferences.

Meanwhile, the Abuja talks of 2 - 3 May 2001 had ensured that peace held out in Sierra Leone, while the cease-fire helped in the disarmament, demobilization and re-integration of former fighters and estranged Sierra Leoneans. The Talks also further enabled the deployment of UNAMSIL deep into RUF controlled territories.[34] The long and short-term lesson from the Sierra Leonean civil war was that peace-building measures are necessary to prevent a similar macabre scenario being enacted in Africa or in any other part of the world. In Sierra Leone, a short statement, 'Never Again', aptly depicted the feelings of many, an exclamation that was made by an RUF fighter who returned home only to realise the devastation the civil war had wrought. This statement later gave birth to a Non-Governmental Organisation.

The major challenge to the newly elected Kabbah government (it again won the elections held in May 2002) remained to be able to promote the rule of law and the establishment of institutions of justice in the midst of the public outcry for revenge and remorse for those accused of human rights abuses during the war. Another challenge was for the government to be tolerant and inclusive of all segments of the Sierra Leonean society with nationalist outlook in the political process.

The national army and police need to be restructured and retrained; the legal and judicial systems need to be reformed and strengthened. There should also be an assessment of national law enforcement and judicial institutions, including the physical damage caused by the conflict, so that the necessary assistance may be provided to enable these institutions to ensure long-term protection of human rights and the restoration of the rule of law. Some countries like Nigeria are already providing assistance towards the training and equipment of the new Sierra Leonean army. They should ensure that this assistance also include effective training in international human rights and humanitarian law.[35] Children who have been both victims and perpetrators of human rights abuses in Sierra Leone deserve special attention.

In summary, we should note that both the wars in Liberia and Sierra Leone have a historical and political basis that should not be overlooked. The wars should be understood in relation to the respective social, economic and historical contexts of each country. We should also try to understand how experiences related to corruption, violence (political and economic) and deepening poverty formed the social experience of generations of young people over time.[36] According to Boas[37] the RUF and the other armed groups, whether Kamajors or NPFL may have more in common than what actually separates them. In a way one is wont to suggest that the wars in Liberia and Sierra Leone were fundamentally 'youth wars' or even 'generational wars'.[38] This is because the historical legacies of the two countries led to a whole generation of young men and women developing a lifestyle of violence, war, and looting built on a common cosmology of joint experiences of social exclusion. Therefore, in order to be able to address the issues of rehabilitation and reconciliation holistically, we must begin to dissect the historical moorings of the conflict. This can only be done on a sustainable basis through applying peace building measures. The related dimension of the exportation of conflicts within the sub-region and the implications for peace as a whole becomes even more pertinent as attempts continue towards designing sustainable regional and holistic interventions for peace.

For Sierra Leone, as the United Nation's Mission in the country fast diminishes, the immediate priority remains how to re-organize and empower the security apparatus in such a way that it is able to police and ensure security in the whole country. Over the longer term, the underlying causes of the conflict must be addressed, while economic opportunities need to be created for the youths and better relations built with the neighbouring countries. Overall, it can be said, that Sierra Leone is a success story of a post-conflict and peace-building experiment.

Notes

1. Timo Kivimaki & Liisa Laakso (eds.). *Greed, Grievance and Weak States: Overview of African Conflicts*, Helsinki, Department of Political Science and Department of Development Studies, 2000, p.186.
2. Morten Boas 'Liberia and Sierra Leone - dead ringers? The logic of neopatrimonial rule', *Third World Quarterly*, Vol.22, No.5, 2001, p.713.
3. Ibid, p.714.
4. Eric G. Berman and Katie E. Sams, *Peacekeeping in Africa: Capabilities and Culpabilities*, Geneva, UNIDIR, 2002, p.112.
5. Morten Boas, Ibid. p.715.
6. Morten Boas, Bid, p.716.
7. Ferme, Mariane, 'The Violence of Numbers: Consensus, Competition and the Negotiation of Disputes in Sierra Leone', *Cahiers d'Etudes Africaines*, 150 - 152, XXXVIII, 1998, pp.555 - 580.

8. Alfred B. Zack-Williams, 'Sierra Leone: The Political Economy of Civil War, 1991 - 98', *Third World Quarterly*, 20:1, pp.143 - 162.
9. The British were mainly concerned with protecting the mineral resources in Sierra Leone in its competition with France in the sub-region at minimal cost.
10. *Africa Confidential*, 20 October 1999, 6 February, 1998.
11. Joe C. Blell, Sierra Leonean Ambassador to Nigeria, Lecture by his Excellency on 'Nigeria-Sierra Leone bilateral relations as well as current developments in Sierra Leone', Nigerian Institute of International Affairs, Lagos, June 1999, p.1
12. IRIN, 6 August 1999.
13. Robin Hay, *Peace-building During Peace Support Operations: A Survey and Analysis of Recent Missions*, Canada, Department of Foreign Affairs and International Trade, March 14, 1999, p.7.
14. Ibid, p.9.
15. IRIN-West Africa Update 373, 5 January 1999. See also Ehichioya Ezomon, Sola Dixon, and Moses Ayo Jolayemi, 'Britain Spends N4.5 billion on Sierra Leone says Cook', *The Guardian* (Lagos), 11 March 1999, pp.1-2.
16. Timo Kivimaki and Liisa Laakso, op cit.., p.190.
17. IRIN-West Africa, 28 March, 2002.
18. Catherine Barnes & Tara Polzer, *Sierra Leone Peace Process: Learning from the Past to Address Current Challenges*, An Expert Seminar Report, London, and 27 September, 2000. This Report can be found on the Internet at http://www.c-r.org/occ-papers/S/semreport.html.
19. Ibid.
20. Ibid.
21. British Army, *Wider Peacekeeping, The Army Field Manual*, Vol.5, Operations Other than War, Part 11, 1981.
22. Mark Molam et.al., *Peacekeeping in Sierra Leone: UNAMSIL Hits the Home Front*, Pretoria, Institute of Security Studies 2002, p.50.
23. Francis Kai-Kai, 'Disarmament, Demobilisation and Re-integration in Post-war Sierra Leone', Anatole Ayissi and Robin-Edward Paulton (eds.), *Bound to Cooperate: Conflict, Peace and People in Sierra Leone*, Geneva, UNIDIR, 2000, p.123.
24. David Lord, Early Civil Society Peace Initiatives, ACCORD, Internet Site: http://www.c-r.ors/accords/s-leone/accorda/early.htm.Visited August 2004.
25. Thomas Mark Turay, Civil Society and Peace-building: The role of the Inter-Religious Council of Sierra Leone, Internet site: http: www.c-r.org/accord/s-leone/accora/society.htm. Visited August 2004.
26. The World Bank, *Peace, Recovery and Development in Sierra Leone*, New York, The World Bank Group, 2004.
27. The World Bank, Ibid.
28. Agence France-Presse (AFP), 18 September, 2001. See also the site: http://www.Sierra-Leone.org/trc.html.
29. Amnesty International, *SIERRA LEONE: Recommendations to the International Contact group on Sierra Leone,* New York, April 19, 1999, p.2.
30. Ibid.

31. *Human Rights Watch,* 1998. See Internet Site: http://ww.hrw.org/reports98/Sierra/ Sierra 88-01.htm#p88 _2288.

32. Femmes Africa Solidarite, *Women's Participation in the Peace Process in Sierra Leone,* Switzerland, AGL FM Production, 1997, p.34.

33. Ibid.

34. Peter Umar-Omole, 'Obasanjo, Konare, Kabbah Hail Truce in Sierra Leone', *THISDAY Newspaper* (Nigeria), vol.7, no.2299, 2001.

35. Amnesty International, 1999, p.6.

36. Martin Boas, 2001, p.718.

37. Ibid.

38. Ibrahim Abdullah, *Between Democracy and Terror: The Sierra Leone Civil War,* Dakar, CODESRIA, 2004.

5

The Guinean Dimension: Dynamics of the Sub-regional Conflicts and Implications for Peace

Another very important dimension to the intermittent conflicts in West Africa is the dovetailing nature of these conflicts or what has been referred to as the 'exportation of war'. The role or possible role that Guinea may have played in exacerbating the conflicts in this region is worth examining. It is indeed very interesting to note that Guinea consistently accused Liberia of sponsoring rebels and trying to destabilize its own government. Liberia in turn, accused Guinea of supporting dissidents, primarily the rebel group known as Liberians United for Reconstruction and Democracy (LURD) that had been trying to overthrow the Taylor government. The Liberian government then maintained that LURD who had periodically attacked Lofa County since 1999 and even approached the outskirts of Monrovia in their attacks were based in and supported by Guinea. On the other hand, Sierra Leone also did accuse Liberia of having sponsored the Revolutionary United Front (RUF) against its government during the bloody Sierra Leonean war.

Guinea, which has a population of about 7.2 million people according to the 1996 census, and a landmass of 245,857 sq. kilometres or 94,926 sq. miles, is made up significantly of the Mandingo population. Alhaji Koromah, leader of ULIMO-K during the Liberian civil war is a Mandingo by birth, and thus it is to be expected that he should have strong cultural if not political ties with Guinea. In fact, President Taylor at a stage protested the alleged training of Mandingo rebels in Guinea. Suffice it to say that, on the other hand, Guinea had an overt distrust of Côte d'Ivoire, which it accused of supporting Charles

Taylor. In retrospect, let us recall that whatever their distaste for Samuel Doe, Guinea and Sierra Leone probably for internal security reasons, maintained relatively friendly relations with Doe. These countries were then inundated with Liberian refugees during the Liberian war, many of whom were Doe's allies.

For the three countries, Liberia, Sierra Leone and Guinea that make up the Mano River Union, what is immediately common about these countries is the geographical proximity of each to the other. Another common observation, which is even more pertinent, is the availability of abundant natural and mineral resources in the area. Hence, very valuable resources like timber, iron one, rubber, diamonds and gold could be found in commercial quantities. The implication is that the desire to control, exploit and export these resources meant the frequent movement and intermingling of their citizens, especially those living in and around the border areas. Again, the scheming and jostling of some of the actors, including governments, foreign agents and even mercenaries were to some extent, to be in a position to benefit directly or indirectly from the exploitation of these resources. This had meant some sort of competition, and therefore increased conflicts with the ultimate aim of being able to control and access the mineral-rich areas in these countries. Of course, this had its political costs as the events unfolded. For instance, it had been observed that the conflict in the region was exacerbated when Taylor on taking over in Liberia refused to honour his promise of allowing his Sierra Leonean allies access to more minerals in Liberia.

It was fairly common knowledge that the Liberian government was involved in the Sierra Leonean war, and that this constituted a serious impediment to the political transition programme in Sierra Leone. It appeared that the Liberian government at a time assisted in the training and arming of the RUF, which was then fighting to unseat the elected government of Tejan Kabba in Sierra Leone.

On the other hand, it had been suggested that the armed incursions of dissidents in the north-western (Lofa county) of Liberia could be attributed to Liberian rebels recruited in Sierra Leone, but who felt excluded from the political process by the manner the Lome peace process had been implemented by the Taylor government. Indeed, Lofa County had experienced more internal strife and external attacks from the Guinea border, which led to the massive displacement of its population, including thousands of Sierra Leonean refugees.[1]

Considerations of strategic interest would seem to indicate a motive for Guinea or even Sierra Leone to seek to intervene in Liberia under serious conflict of interests. A critical observation of the Liberian imbroglio and the Sierra

Leonean conflict would seem to indicate that Charles Taylor had played a not too palatable role in the destabilization of Sierra Leone for several reasons, while antagonising Guinea by his constant accusations. One of these reasons would be his desire to access directly or indirectly the diamond-rich areas of Sierra Leone, while another will be to keep the Sierra Leonean government busy fighting rebels instead of causing havoc in his backyard.

Subsequently, in response to the accusations by the Taylor government in 2000 of Sierra Leone's possible involvement in the resurgence of conflict in Liberia, principally by the LURD rebels, the Sierra Leonean government officially noted that, 'it does not support any attempt by rebels to unseat the legitimate government of President Charles Taylor'. This notwithstanding, the Liberian government disclosed that some of the captured rebel fighters were from the disarmed *Kamajors* or Civil Defense Forces of Sierra Leone. However, the same government was to observe, that this did not necessarily mean that the Kabbah government in Sierra Leone supported the activities of the captured Sierra Leonean rebels.

As was the case with the Sierra Leonean government, Guinea also claimed 'it was not interested in war with Liberia'. Despite this disclaimer, it was difficult for President Lansana Conte of Guinea to distance himself from the activities of Sekou Conneh, LURD's national chairman, who is said to be his son-in-law, and who nursed the ambition of becoming President of Liberia. Also, it appeared that Conte adopted a hardline posture towards Liberian refugees who sought refuge in his country. The reason being that he had engaged in negotiations with Samuel Doe concerning future mining of iron ore in Guinea in which Guinea would be allowed to utilize the railway in Liberia built by LAMCO, a Swedish American Liberian Consortium. This was to allow Guinea ship its iron ore through the port of Buchanan in Liberia at an affordable tariff rate. In addition, Conte might have thought that allowing refugees into Guinea might encourage violent opposition and attempts against his government.

On the resurgence of conflict in Liberia, a significant number of Liberians did not support the LURD rebel advance to Monrovia, but would rather prefer that the differences be ironed out through dialogue, preferably through a national conference. In fact, an organization called Mandingo Organized for Democracy in Liberia (MODEL), viewed the action by LURD, of trying to march into Monrovia, as 'uncivilized, barbaric and totally inhumane'. Whatever the case, the point remained that the Sub-region could not afford another major conflict in the Mano River Union. This was indeed, a challenge for ECOWAS, for Nigeria and those who wanted to see the Liberia peace process succeed. Even the European Union welcomed the dialogue which subsequently took place amongst the Mano River Union Countries (Liberia, Sierra Leone and Guinea), but especially the decision to oppose forces seeking to destabilize the region, the establishment of joint border patrols and taking action against the proliferation of small arms.[2] A subsequent meeting was held in Morocco, April 2002, by the foreign ministers of the three countries to review progress towards ensuring peace in the sub-region and to plan a summit of their heads of states.[3]

The dynamics, in terms of the dovetailing nature of conflicts amongst the Mano River Union Countries, therefore tasks the repertoire of measures capable of enhancing the simultaneous reconstruction and reconciliation of their war-torn societies. As was rightly put by Berman and Sams,[4] the end of the cold war has altered the international peace and security landscape significantly. Traditional peacekeeping has now been further extended to include both peace-enforcement and post-cold war peace operations, involving not only economic and humanitarian concerns but also political and social components. For the United Nations, the principles of consent, impartiality and defensive force are no longer the hallmarks of UN operations in conflict situations. Indeed, missions had been established where consent was forfeited, impartiality was forgone, and force had been used other than in self-defence. It was therefore understandable, even justifiable, especially from the humanitarian angle, why the threat to sub-regional security posed by the Liberian and Sierra Leonean crises necessitated a peacekeeping and later, peace-enforcement action by the Nigerian-led ECOMOG forces.

For Nigeria, its leadership of ECOMOG marked a turning point in its diplomatic history as a regional power in Africa. As has been well argued by many, Nigeria had a moral duty to contain the threat posed by the Liberian civil war in the sub-region. This was possible and necessary because of its size, economic and military capability in contrast to those of other countries in the sub-region. According to Sanda,[5] Nigeria took up the gauntlet (as in the days of the anti-colonial apartheid struggle) to intervene in Liberia, bravely breaking new grounds in conflict management at the regional level, which was a decision in keeping with her oft-stated posture as 'big brother' on the continent. Increasingly, the country is being perceived as a benign hegemon within the continent.

It suffices to observe that in a world of growing interdependence among nations, the principle of non-interference in the internal affairs of other countries as canvassed by the then OAU has become an anachronism. This observation has been given practical recognition by the African Union which stipulated that selected member states could be allowed to engage in peace enforcement action in any country where there is serious conflict. In fact, this is also in recognition by many countries that in today's inter-state relations, the cartographic boundary of a country is not necessarily coterminous with the security boundary of the state.[6] However, this penchant for intervening in other countries has not been without its economic costs. In short, this is also one of the most important considerations when countries decide to engage in peace enforcement missions in another country. For Nigeria, President Obasanjo in 1999 disclosed that the country had expended close to US8 billion on ECOMOG with the loss of about 1,000 of its soldiers.[7] This notwithstanding, many are wont to concur with the United Nations when it noted, that 'compared to war, peacekeeping (peace support operations) consumes far fewer resources; war costs in just one day what keeping the peace costs in a year'.[8]

As was suggested by Terhi Lehtinen,[9] there is the absolute necessity to seriously review the overall policy in this region in order to address economic, social, security and political grievances in Liberia and the neighbouring countries in a more coordinated manner. The efforts of the Mano River women network, made up of influential women seeking to pave way for lasting peace, and the decision of the Mano River Union to also to set up border patrols, involve the people, discourage the proliferation of arms and ammunition, repatriate refugees, share intelligence and educate their people on the value of promoting a culture of peace are all in the right direction.

A critical appraisal of conflicts in the region should include finding solution to the resurgence of armed conflicts in Liberia because of its negative implications for countries like Guinea and Sierra Leone. This presupposes that only a comprehensive plan or approach geared towards stabilizing the border regions of the three countries simultaneously would ensure lasting peace and development in the Mano River Basin.

Notes

1. IRIN, August 1991.
2. 'Can Mano River Union Countries Achieve Peace?' The Perspective, Smyma, George, August 30, 2001.
3. IRIN, 8 April, 2002.
4. Eric, G. Berman and Katie, E. Sams, Peace Keeping in Africa: Capabilities and Culpabilities, United Nations, 2000, p.31.
5. Julie Sanda, 'Peace Making in Nigeria's Foreign Policy: 1999 2003, Bola A. Akinterinwa (ed.), Nigeria's New Foreign Policy Thrust: Essays in Honour of Ambassador Oluyemi Adeniji, Ibadan, Vantage Publishers, 2004, p.271.
6. Solomon, O. Ogwu, 'Nigeria and the Liberian Imbroglio: An Epitome of Nigerian-led Crisis Resolution in the Sub-Region, Nigerian Forum, Vol.13, Nos.9 - 10, September-October, 1994, p.199.

7.*Punch* (Lagos), 26 October, 1999, pp.1-2. According to *The Guardian* (Nigeria), of July 7, 2004, p.15, Nigeria spent N8.4 billion in the Liberian operation. Averagely, $1 US exchanged for N100. Of 3,310 troops sent by West Africa, Nigeria contributed 1,580. The remaining troops were from Ghana, Gambia, Guinea Bissau, Mali, Senegal and Togo.

8.United Nations, *United Nations' Peace Keeping*, New York: UN Department of Public Information, 1996, p.6.

6

Other Conflicts in the Sub-Region

Apart from the better-known conflicts in Liberia, Sierra Leone and Guinea, there were also other pockets of conflicts, which created problems for peace and security in the West African sub-region. These include the conflicts in Guinea-Bissau, Côte d'Ivoire, and Senegal, in the Casamance region. Of interest, is the fact that many of these conflicts were internal in nature or domestically contained, revolving around issues of access to power, marginalization, citizenship and identity and resource allocation. Even Nigeria, the regional bridge builder, also has to contend with a myriad of conflicts within the territory. This has been able to do so far as failure to do so has serious implications for peace and stability in the sub-region.

Guinea Bissau

Take the Guinea-Bissau civil war for instance, which lasted from June to October 1998. The war basically concerned the distribution of institutional political power against the background of the perceived illegitimacy of President Nino Viera's rule. The immediate cause of the war however, was the dismissal of Army Chief of Staff General Ansumane Mane, which led to an uprising by army officers on 7 June 1998. Viera had suspended Mane in January that year on the accusation that he had been involved in supplying arms to the Casamance Separatists fighting the Senegalese government. Mane maintained his innocence, and the government set up a parliamentary inquiry into the accusation. However, before the inquiry could make its findings known, Vieira replaced Mane with General Humberto Gomes and the army staged a coup d'état in retaliation.[1] Citing bilateral defence accords, Guinea and Senegal intervened militarily in Guinea-Bissau in support of Viera, thereby exacerbating the conflict. Whilst the Casamance dimension prompted Senegal's interven-

tion, Guinea may have been concerned about the implications of refugee in-
flux into its territory, apart from the observation that the Guinea president,
Lansana Conteh, is said to be a close friend to Veira.[2]

It is interesting to recall that both Nino Viera and Ansumane Mane were
comrades in arms against Portuguese colonial rule in the 1970s, though they
represented two different factions in the struggle for independence.[3] The conflict
between Viera and his supporters and Mane and his supporters who were
predominantly from the Guinea-Bissau Army continued until August 1999,
when under the joint aegis of ECOWAS and *Communidade Dos Paises de Lingua
Portuguesa* (CPLP), a cease-fire agreement was brokered in July 1998. The cease-
fire called for the deployment of observation and inter-position forces.[4] Also,
there was a National Reconciliation conference in August 1999, which brought
together some 300 representatives of political and civil society groups calling
for the demobilization of the military and free and fair election.[5]

In the November 1998 Abuja Accord, Viera and Mane agreed to the total
withdrawal of foreign troops from Guinea-Bissau. The Peace Agreement at
Abuja also called for a 600-man ECOMOG force to police the withdrawal of
Guinean and Senegalese soldiers and the subsequent elections. Prior to this
period, Guinea and Senegalese forces were stationed in Guinea-Bissau. After
the coup, which deposed President Viera, Portugal which had been more
sympathetic to the rebel cause,[6] offered him asylum and he was allowed to
leave Guinea-Bissau. The Prime Minister designate who was appointed to head
the transitional government of national unity reportedly claimed that the
presence of Guinean and Senegalese troops endangered the fragile peace in
the country. In fact, the final withdrawal of Guinean and Senegalese troops
was only completed at the end of March 1999.[7]

In terms of the conflict resolution efforts, the UN Security Council
condemned the coup in Guinea-Bissau and strongly opposed the use of force
for non-constitutional purposes. The UN also commended the efforts made by
ECOWAS to restore peace in Guinea-Bissau. It subsequently set up the United
Nations Peace Building Office in Guinea-Bissau (UNOGBIS),[8] to enhance
reconciliation, strengthen democratic institutions and develop an integrated
approach to peace building programmes. In October 2001, the mandate of
UNOGBIS was extended until December 2002. The Organization of Africa Unity
(OAU) also condemned the May 7 military coup and demanded for the
restoration of constitutional legality and respect for the Abuja Agreement.[9]
Basically, ECOWAS took the leading role in the mediation of the Guinea-Bissau conflict. Its plan called for a cease-fire, the establishment of a government
of National Unity and the withdrawal of all foreign troops to be simultaneously

accompanied by the deployment of ECOMOG.[10] ECOMOG eventually deployed when Togo dispatched an advance detachment of some 110 military personnel in December 1998. By 12 February, a 600-strong battalion comprised of equal numbers of troops from Benin, the Gambia, Niger, and Togo was in place.[11]

For the first time, it appeared that ECOMOG operated in accordance with a clearly defined mandate. A legal framework signed between ECOWAS and representatives of the two parties to the conflict dated 22 March 1999 was produced.[12] Also, the ECOMOG force in Guinea-Bissau signalled an improvement from previous initiatives. The often bandied charge that ECOMOG was an instrument of Nigeria's foreign policy in the sub-region collapsed. This time around, the force comprised of one anglophone and three francophone countries. Guinea and Senegal, two ECOWAS member states were expressly forbidden from participating in this operation because the military junta to the conflict objected to their presence. This was the first time that a demand by a party to a major conflict with respect to force composition was heeded[13].

In summary, there was a fundamental contradiction in the conflicting parties' conception of the nature of this conflict. Viera's government represented itself as being democratically elected, and loyalist forces as fighting to restore order, while Mane insisted on the shortcomings of the government, and questioned the continued legitimacy of Viera. The rebels therefore believed, rightly or wrongly, that their objective was to reorganize a collapsed state authority.[14]

In the elections of November 1999, The Party for Social Renewal (PSR), the opposition, was victorious winning 37 out of a total of 102 seats.[15] In January 2000, Kumba Yalls was elected president with 72 percent of the vote, however, many, including the international community were concerned about the potential for renewed conflict due to ethnic tensions, insecurity and indiscipline in some segments of the army. That the international community through ECOWAS and the UN acted promptly cannot be denied. Again, the point is made that serious wars can be prevented when concerted action is taken under a multilateral framework, provided that the parties to the conflict show enough political will to restore peace.

Though, Guinea-Bissau succumbed to another coup in September 2003, considerable progress has since been made towards bringing back democracy. The country has successfully held legislative elections, a major step towards restoring constitutional order and promoting sustainable peace and security. While the Presidential election is scheduled for 2005, the government still grapples with the problem of salary arrears and accessing resources to jump start economic development. The United Nations appear to have recognized the positive developments in Guinea-Bissau, and is being called upon to extend more technical and financial assistance to the troubled country.

Senegal and the Casamance Conflict

The conflict between the Senegalese government and the Casamance rebels has been going on for nearly two decades. However, a cease-fire agreement was signed between the leader of the *Mouvement des Forces Démocratiques de la Casamance* (MFDC) led by the cleric, Diamacoune Senghor and President Abdoulaye Wade of Senegal on November 30, 2000.[16] At the 47th Ordinary Session of the ECOWAS Heads of State meeting held in the Malian Capital Bamako, ECOWAS commended President Abdoulaye Wade for his peace moves in initiating dialogue with the separatist fighters in Casamance.

In retrospect, the MFDC took up arms in 1982 demanding independence for the tourist and agricultural province which has its provincial capital at Ziguinchor. The MFDC claimed that the central government of Senegal had neglected this part of the country for a long time. Since 1991, the MFDC signed several cease-fire agreements, all of which collapsed. Fighting flared up again in 2000, and in the incident, two people were killed by a group of armed men believed to be MFDC rebels. On coming to power in March 2000 through an electoral victory, Abdoulaye Wade of Senegal pledged to make the resolution of the Casamance conflict a priority.

Because this conflict had affected some of Senegal's neighbours like Gambia and Guinea-Bissau, many of the talks on resolving the conflict usually included delegations from these countries. Both Gambia and Guinea-Bissau were said to have served as military bases for the MFDC.[17] This did not of course mean that their governments were in support of the rebellion. It is said that the Casamance separatists had funded their activities by trading cannabis for arms across the Senegal-Guinea Bissau border.[18] This smuggling of arms and Cannabis across the border had purportedly been going on for years. Further, Guinea-Bissau military sent to secure the border often gradually became drawn into the lucrative arms-cannabis smuggling racket.[19] The conflict therefore, has regional implications in terms of its dynamics. For instance, it was observed that deposed President Viera had committed himself since 1995 to fighting the rebellion at the border region in order to be absorbed into the CFA franc zone thus endangering the cross-border traffic in arms in which many army officers were involved. This had been variously cited as one of the reasons why the Guinea-Bissau Army rose against him. For now, the emphasis of both parties to the conflict, the Senegalese government as well as the MFDC, is the consolidation of the cease-fire agreement, disarmament and the release of prisoners. Apart from the peace Agreement earlier signed, the MFDC was swayed in its decision to broker peace by the death in 2003 of Sidi Badji, a hardline guerrilla leader of MFDC opposed to any deal with the Senegalese government, by a conference of the MFDC which called for a peace settlement with the authorities in Dakar. A total of 50,000 people had been displaced from their homes as a result of the rebellion, with about 6,000 in Guinea Bissau and 5,000 in Gambia. With peace in sight as at 2004, about 15,000 people were expected to return to their home villages as the low-level insurgency that had gone on for about 22 years peters off. Despite recent signs that peace is slowly returning to the area, there still remains the legacy of displaced persons and the threat of landmines.

The Senegalese government in partnership with the UNDP is working together in the post-conflict environment in the Casamance region to enthrone some semblance of development. Whilst the United Nations has pledged a donation of $4.5 million to reduce poverty in the area, the Senegalese government is increasing efforts in rehabilitating infrastructure, providing social services, creating local businesses and resettling displaced farmers that are returning home. Though this conflict lasted for so long, the efforts being made by the Senegalese government and the United Nations and the modest gains achieved, indicate that sustainable peace can only be attained through an approach that is not only comprehensive but also, includes the neighbouring countries.

The Uprising in Côte d'Ivoire

Generally, Côte d'Ivoire had over the years been known as a stable, if not the most stable country in the West African region until recently. This stability was shattered by political, social and economic crises, which besieged the country from 1999 to 2000, and led to a coup d'état in December 1999. In retrospect, Côte d'Ivoire which was part of French West Africa became independent in 1960, with the long shadow of the statesman and 'founding father', Felix Houphouët-Boigny ever on the horizon. Since his death in December 1993, there had been the subtlest of power struggles amongst the political class over what may be regarded as Houphouët-Boigny's heritage.[20]

It is said that the abuse of power, corruption, economic decline and especially Boigny's successor, Henri Konan Bedie's xenophobic ideology of 'Ivoirité', paved the way for a fatal political impasse. The political conflict erupted when President Bedie refused his rival Alassane Ouattara's candidature in the presidential elections in 2000, on the basis of his alleged foreign origin. A coup d'état was finally triggered by a military uprising, following the non-payment of soldiers' salaries. Quite suddenly, the capital, Abidjan, became a scene of violence, which led to political and economic chaos and the eventual deposition of President Bedie.[21] Most interesting was the fact, that the Ivorian population largely supported the coup d'état, with the media qualifying it as a 'social revolution'.[22]

Let us recall that Côte d'Ivoire was ruled as a one-party state whilst ethnic differences were largely effectively underplayed. Houphouët-Boigny as a matter of policy opened the frontiers of Côte d'Ivoire to foreigners from all over the world, especially the poor and troubled countries of West Africa, Liberia, Sierra Leone, Nigeria, Niger, Benin, Burkina Faso and Mali. Though, this all-embracing policy was implemented in such a way that it did not affect the country negatively, some Ivorians complained about what they considered to be foreign invasion. However, in a situation of a one party rule, they could do very little about it. Therefore, under President Bedie, the rather ethnicist policy of 'Ivoirité' was perceived by many as undesirable, especially if it tended to justify nepotism and exclusion of other groups in the Ivorian society. Subsequently, the debate on nationality threatened to divide the country along ethnic lines, hitherto suppressed.

Mercifully, the events leading up to the coup resulted in very few victims, except the widespread pillage and insecurity throughout Abidjan, the economic capital.[23] The military however, had complete control of the country, partly as a way to reassure the international community that there was still stability in the country. The military created the *Comité National du Salut Public* (CNSP), to form the government in the transitional period. The transitional government and the main opposition parties, the *Rassemblement des Républicains* (RDR) and the *Front Populaire Ivoirien* (FPI), were constituted 4 January 2000. General Guei, the leader of the coup d'état, set up the Constitutional and Electoral Commission and promised to complete the electoral process by October 2000. By July 2000, a constitutional referendum was held and a new constitution was adopted even though acts of violence still continued. The New constitution set up strict nationality rules for presidential candidates.[24] The Referendum of 24 July 2000 was endorsed by 86.7 percent of the countries 4.8 million voters.[25] Meanwhile, ousted President Bedie, who sought for ECOWAS to intervene, received a negative response, as many ECOWAS countries felt that he did not merit any assistance.

On 6 October 2000 the Côte d'Ivoire Supreme Court disqualified not only the experienced but controversial politician, Alassane Ouattara, but also all the five rival candidates of the former ruling party, the PDCI *(Parti Démocrati-*

que de la Côte d'Ivoire). Only five of the presidential candidates were approved, including General Guei, head of the military junta, and Laurent Gbagbo, a veteran opposition leader and head of the FPI. The disqualification of PDCI candidates meant that the presidential elections would be held without the participation of the party, which won 96 percent of votes in the 1995 exercise.[26] Subsequently, it was ironical that General Guei, who deposed the PDCI from power, decided to run for the presidency under the same party's ticket. Meanwhile, the economic fortunes of Côte d'Ivoire continued to dwindle, thereby creating a lot of problem for the transitional government. For instance, the international financial institutions suspended assistance to Côte d'Ivoire, whilst the price of cocoa, of which Côte d'Ivoire was a number one producer, dropped. General Guei, himself was initially lucky, as he managed to survive two coups d'état from within the military during this period.

An OAU Committee of Ten attempted to design a solution to the Ivorian conflict, without any success. However, after ten months of transitional rule by the military, the elections of 22 October 2000 narrowed down to a contest between General Guei and Laurent Gbagbo of the *Front Populaire Ivoirien* (FPI). After a rather controversial counting of the votes, both candidates declared themselves winners at various times in the process. Demonstrations began in several big cities, a curfew was announced and a state of emergency declared. In the end, the electoral commission, *Commission Nationale Electorale* (CNE), declared Laurent Gbagbo winner with 59.36 percent votes as against 32.7 percent for General Robert Guei.[27] According to official reports, the post-election violence left in its wake a death toll of 171 and several injured. The President in his solidarity message to the nation, declared a day of national mourning.

For Côte d'Ivoire, which had been touted as the most stable country in West Africa for so long, this experience of violence and deaths was to say the least traumatic. It is however, expected that the peace so far regained would be further consolidated by the election of representatives to the legislature. The lesson from the Ivorian conflict is how not to allow ambition and elite disunity destroy what had been built over a long period.

There were however, two important developments in 2002, which appeared to point a way forward for Côte d'Ivoire. Laurent Gbagbo formed a Government of National Unity, and awarded Mr. Ouattara a certificate of Ivorian nationality. However, this gesture was eclipsed when soldiers said to have been recruited during General Guei's tenure in office staged a mutiny which led to the death of General Guei, his family members and his supporters. Many Ivorians considered to be immigrants were subsequently chased out of the country by government forces and its supporters.

The response to this was the emergence of a coalition of rebel forces known as the *Mouvement Patriotique de Côte d'Ivoire* (MPCI), led by a former student leader, Guillame Soro. Before long, two more anti-Gbagbo parties also emerged. *Mouvement Populaire Ivoirien du Grand Ouest* (MPIGO), and the Movement for Justice and Peace (MP), both claiming the immediate objective of fighting to avenge Mr. Guei's death. In short, the country was divided into two, with peacekeeping forces from the UN Operation in Côte d'Ivoire (ONUCI) stationed between the opposition- held north and government- controlled south.

As usual, ECOWAS did not relent in its peace efforts in the sub-region. A 2003 peace Agreement, the Linas-Marcoussis Agreement ended the fighting in the country. But, still peace was far from being achieved in the country. A new pact signed in Accra, known as the Accra III Agreement called for the establishment of a monitoring group that would submit a progress report every two weeks to the United Nations, ECOWAS and the African Union (AU). The parties to the conflict made new pledges on matters of eligibility of a presidential candidate, disarmament, demobilization and reintegration process (DDR) for the rebel combatants, and delegation of some of the powers by the president to the Prime Minister until elections scheduled for October 2005. Again, ECOWAS and the United Nations did what they were expected to do. However, the point remains that for lasting peace to be achieved in Côte d'Ivoire, constitutional remedies and the political will must be found for the rather stubborn 'nationality' question in this once peaceful and stable country. The efforts being made by ECOWAS and the United Nations should be commended as the crisis in Côte d'Ivoire has implications for peace amongst its neighbours, namely, Liberia, Ghana, Guinea, Burkina Faso and Mali. Indeed, the fact that Côte d'Ivoire is home to thousands of nationals from all over the sub-region including Nigeria, makes the resolution of its conflict a regional issue.

Myriad of Conflicts in Nigeria

In the case of Nigeria, which is politically and economically a strong regional player in West Africa, it has been a case of intermittent conflicts, mainly ethnic, religious and communal conflicts of low-intensity. Since its political independence in 1960, and the end of a bloody civil war (1967-1970), the country has been quite wary of allowing any conflict to assume deadly proportions. Considering it immense size of 356, 669 sq. miles or 923,768 sq. km, a population of over 120 million with about 250 ethnic groups,[28] it is to be expected that conflicts may indeed, arise from time to time.

Within the past two decades, the country has witnessed a myriad of conflicts, like the ethnic conflicts in Zango-Kataf and Tafawa Balewa in the north; Ife-

Modekeke conflict in the Southwest; the Umuleri-Aguleri conflict in the Southeast; the Tivs versus Jukuns in the central region; and several religious riots and conflicts in towns like Kaduna, Kano, Sagamu and Aba.[29] Further, the activities of ethnic militias in several parts of the country have in recent times, also led to serious concerns about general insecurity in the country and the implication of this for the stability of the country and the sub-region. Some of the militias amongst several that are visible in the Nigerian fourth democratic environment include the Egbesu Boys of the Niger Delta Area, Oodua Peoples Congress (OPC) of the Southwest, the Bakassi Boys and Movement for the Actualisation of the Sovereign State of Biafra (MASSOB) of the Southeast and the Arewa Peoples Congress (APC) of the North. In 2005 and early 2006, a new group known as the Movement for the Emancipation of the Niger-Delta (MEND) arose in the oil producing area and gave the Nigerian state sleepless nights by blowing up oil facilities and kidnapping foreign oil workers. Each claims to be representing and protecting the ethnic interests of their people.[30] Today, the activities of these militias if unchecked, and the associated political violence and the impunity of the political parties in denying Nigerians their rightful votes constitute serious threats to the country's democracy. For instance, it is common knowledge that the 2003 elections in Nigeria largely won by the Peoples Democratic Party (PDP) was seriously flawed right from the party primaries to the elections proper. In several instances, many Nigerians were denied of their votes and had people imposed on them other than their candidates. The revelations at the Election Tribunals in Anambra State and Ogun State are cases in point. Generally, political and communal violence have increased in the country since the May 1999 successful elections to civil governance. The volatile oil rich Niger-Delta has continued to experience violence while in the north of the country, the introduction of the 'Sharia' (Strict Islamic Law) created the potential for increased violence between the Christians and Moslems or in fact, more religious riots in the foreseeable future.

In retrospective, it appears that years of military rule in the country resulted in the entrenchment of corruption and arbitrariness in governance, both very serious social ills. The situation was further complicated by the political dimension which had the political leadership in the country largely dominated and controlled by the military and civilian elite from basically two major geographical areas of the country, the North and the West. The implication of this is easy to imagine. The result was marginalization, alienation and apathy to the Nigerian state of the generality of other Nigerians who considered themselves excluded from governance. So far, the country has initiated various constitutional, structural and institutional reforms, which hopefully will help redress the anomalies characterizing the political structure and the polity. As has been variously argued,[31] it is time for a redesign of the federal system in Nigeria. In fact, the 'National Question' in Nigeria, is still begging for an answer. So far, it appears that the elected politicians are still chasing shadows, preferring to line their pockets first and foremost, rather than squarely addressing the issue of the country's skewed federalism and ultimate survival. These still remain major challenges for the Olusegun Obasanjo's Peoples Democratic Party (PDP) in government since 1999, and re-elected in 2003, and other elected governments that may come after. However, the good news is that the Obasanjo Government in late February 2005 finally agreed to constitute the 'National Political Reform Conference' to enable Nigerians discuss their problems and chart a path for the future. Though speedily constituted, this Conference fell short of the expectations of the civil society who accused the government of hijacking the Sovereign National Conference (SNC) that had for long been demanded by the civil society. Led by Anthony Enahoro, the Pro-National Conference Organisation (PRONACO), a coalition of civil society groups accused the government of insincerity for indirectly appointing about 50 per cent of the total number of delegates to the Conference. They do not therefore see the outcome of the Conference as representing the wishes of ordinary Nigerians. PRONACO refused to participate in the Conference. However, it is important to observe that President Obasanjo, an avowed disciple of federalism and the indivisibility of Nigeria, once more exhibited his characteristic courage by agreeing to the constitution of the Conference to enable Nigerians to talk to each other at this period. Though the Conference would have been more legitimate if it was more inclusive, it nevertheless is a step forward towards seeking ways of redesigning Nigeria for a more stable future.

For now, the country appears to be consolidating its hard-earned democracy. Since second elections have generally been problematic in Africa, there were fears that the transition from civilian to civilian rule in Nigeria would be a violent one. But to everyone's surprise, the country once again proved to the world that it might have come of political age by successfully conducting presidential, gubernatorial and state legislative elections all over the country without widespread violence. The largely violent-free elections could be attributed to the various efforts at political enlightenment by the state, civil society, international community, and government agencies like the Ministry of Information and National Orientation. Though, the country seemed to have weathered this storm, it is still imperative to redress the injustices perpetrated by the ruling party (PDP) in particular against the opposition in terms of vote manipulation, disenfranchisement of the youth and official intimidation in order to avoid a situation in future when such actions may lead to violent resistance. It appeared that Nigerians accepted their lot by reluctantly resorting to the electoral tribunals set up for redressing instances of electoral fraud and manipulation. It is actually instructive that one of the Election Tribunals in one of the component states, Edo State, in its ruling upturned the victory of a purportedly elected member of the PDP to the Federal House of Representatives. There were several other litigations at the Tribunals still unresolved even after almost two years of being instituted. Nonetheless, it appears that democracy is gradually taking root in Nigeria. However, the extent to which the ethnically politicised polity can withstand the multiple political shocks being inflicted on her remains to be seen. So far, it has proven resilient. From all indications, Nigeria appreciates the role it had often played, and intends to continue playing in West Africa. From this perspective, the country and indeed, the sub-region cannot afford to add a conflagration arising from electoral conflicts to the myriad of persisting conflicts in the sub-region. Nigeria also requires assistance in continuous peace-building efforts from other African countries and the International community. This is not just for her, but indeed, for the role she had often had to play in resolving conflicts in the sub-region. The country is set for general elections in 2007 and the Nigerian polity is overheating with many expressing fears of the likely consequences if undemocratic forces were allowed an upper hand as happened in the recent past.

Notes

1 Eric G. Berman and Katie E. Sams, *Peacekeeping in Africa: Capabilities and Culpabilities,* United Nations, UNIDIR, 2000, p.128.

2 'Uprising in Guinea-Bissau', *Africa Research Bulletin,* Vol.35, No.6, 1-30 June, 1998.

3. Terhi Lehtinen, 'The Military-Civilian Crisis in Guinea-Bissau', Timo Kivimaki and Liisa Laakso (eds.) *Greed, Grievance and Weak States: Overview of African Conflicts,* Helsinki, 2000, p.116.

4. UN Document S/1998/825, Annex I, Ceasefire agreement in Guinea-Bissau, I September 1998, Article I (d).

5. IRIN, 18 August, 1999.

6. Alan Rake, 'Will Peace Hold?', *New African,* No.366, September.

7. UN Document S/1999/432, Annex, *Report on the Situation in Guinea-Bissau prepared by the Executive Secretary of ECOWAS,* 16 April 1999, para.8.

8. The UNOGBIS made available US $30,000 for the National Reconciliation conference, held in August 1999 (IRIN, 18 August 1999).

9. PANA, 10 May 1999.

10. PANA, 22 December, 1998.

11. Berman and Sams, op cit.. p.132.

12. UN Document S/1999/445.
13. Berman and Sams, op cit.136.
14. Terhi Lehtinen, op cit. p.120.
15. Timo Kirimaki & Liisa Laakso, op cit, p.22. Se also, UN Security Council, *Speakers in Security Council urge Continued, Coordinated Investment of Peacekeeping, Development Assistance in West Africa*, SC/151, 16 July 2004.
16. 'Senegalese Government, Casamance rebels hold talks', *The Guardian* (Lagos), 18 December, 2000, p.11. Also, ECOWAS deploy troops to Sierra Leave, Guinea, Liberia Borders, *The Punch*, (Lagos), 18 December, 2000, p.6. For an update on the conflict, see UNOCHR, 'Senegal: Help needed for returnees to Casamance', 2004. Internet Site: www://africa.oneworld.net/external/? Visited Agust 2004
17. Ibid.
18. Timo Kivimaki & Liisa, op cit. p.119.
19. Alan Roke, op cit.
20. Terhi Lehtinen, 'The coup d'état in Côte d'Ivoire - The Military as a Guarantor of Civilian Rule?', Timo kivimaki and Lissa Laakso, Op cit. P.89.
21. Ibid.
22. *Jeune Afrique*, January, 2000.
23. Terhi Lehtinen, op cit. p.94.
24. IRIN, July 2000.
25. Paul Michaud, 'Guei, I'm the man', *New African*, No.358, September 2000, p.13.
26. Cersko Omunizua, 'Democracy or "democrazy", *West Africa*, 16-22 October, 2000 p.9.
27. Adrienne Yande Diop, 'Côte d'Ivoire: Learning from Democracy', *The West African Bulletin*, ECOWAS, No.8, December 2000, p.37. For update on the Ivorian crisis, see United Nations, 'Côte d'Ivoire Reconciliation Pact calls for Monitoring Group of UN and Others', Internet site: un.org. /apps/news/ticker/tickerstory.asp?newsID=11611.
28. *Africa, South of the Sahara*, 1999.
29. O. Akintayo & Jane-Frances Agbu, 'Psychological Implications of Ethno-Religious Conflicts in Nigeria', *Nigerian Forum*, July/August, 2002.
30. Osita Agbu, *Ethnic Militias and the Threat to Democracy in Post-Transition Nigeria*, Research Report No. 127, Uppsala, Nordiska Afrikanstitutet, 2004. .
31. Adebayo Olukoshi and Osita Agbu, 'The Deepening Crisis of Nigeria's Federalism and the Future of the Nation-State', Olukoshi and Laakso (eds), *Challenges to the Nation-State in Africa*, Institute of Development Studies, University of Helsinki, Helsinki, 1996. Also, Terhi Lehtinen and Nosakhare Ogumbor, 'The Mosaique of Ethnic and Religious Conflicts in Nigeria', Timo Kivimaki and Liisa Laakso, op cit. p.167. See also, Osita Agbu, 'Re-inventing Federalism in Post-Transition Nigeria: Problems and Prospects', *Africa Development*, Vol.XXIX, No. 2, 2004, pp.27-53.

7

Regional Conflict Resolution Efforts

It is not as if the various conflicts in the West African sub-region have been going on without efforts made at finding solutions to them. However, more often than not, it appears that enough political will was never summoned, generally as a result of the diverse interests of the parties to the conflicts. Oftentimes, African leaders do not seem to have enough political commitment to see the decisions they had taken through. Again, the nature of the conflict resolution mechanisms or approaches left much to be desired. These were often piece-meal and country-specific, when they should have been regional in outlook.

Among the existing approaches to conflict management are such strategies as conflict avoidance, conflict prevention, conflict settlement and conflict resolution. In brief, conflict avoidance refers to efforts to avoid the emergence of contentious issues and the incompatibility of goals between and within actors.[1] On the other hand, conflict prevention refers to measures which contribute to the prevention of undesirable conflict behaviour once some situations involving goal incompatibility has arisen.[2] This entails both short-term and long-term measures. The short-term measures include preventive diplomacy, preventive deployment and preventive disarmament. The long-term measures consist of the various mixes of peace building measures in a post-conflict environment. Further, conflict settlement can be described as a portmanteau term for the ending or termination of conflict, whilst conflict resolution is a somewhat esoteric term for conflict termination. In order to achieve what may be regarded as a resolution, parties to a conflict usually have to redefine their relationship in such a way as to either pursue their goals without conflict or redefine their relationship so that their goals no longer conflict.[4]

In terms of the existing regional conflict resolution strategies in West Africa, these could be classified into two broad categories. These may be called the 'structured' and 'unstructured' mechanisms for conflict resolution and management. The structured strategies are the institutional activities and efforts geared towards conflict resolution and management. These structured strategies are usually very formal and normally take place under the auspices of governmental institutions. Such structured strategies are easily identifiable in the activities of such organisations as the UN, the African Union (AU), *Accord de Non Agression et d'Assistance en matière de Defense* (ANAD), and the Economic Community of West African States (ECOWAS).

The unstructured, on the other hand, as the term suggests, are those strategies evolved not by governmental institutions, but by non-governmental and private organisations in trying to resolve conflicts in the sub-region. In most cases, such unstructured strategies tend to rely more on the attitudinal dispositions of the warring parties in trying to manage the conflict. A quintessential example of such unstructured strategies created especially for the management, if not outright resolution of conflicts in West Africa, was the establishment of the Truth and Reconciliation Commission in Sierra Leone at the conclusion of that country's civil war in 2001. Another good example is what is generally referred to as 'shuttle diplomacy', whereby the combatants are invited by a third party to a neutral country where efforts will be made to resolve the conflict. This was what transpired in Senegal in late 2001 and early 2002, when she invited the two claimants to the Madagascar presidency to come over to 'neutral' Senegal to try and resolve their differences. This was all aimed at avoiding the decline of Madagascar into a costly intra-state conflict.

By observation, both the structured and unstructured strategies tend to be reactive and their relevance is always limited to a particular conflict; and once this has been resolved, it usually becomes obsolete. Both are reactive in the sense that they are merely responses to the conflict – its accompaniment. They only make their presence felt after the conflict must have begun. Also, they are usually based on the twin-concepts of peacekeeping and peace-enforcement. Thus, force is a major component of these strategies. The other features are that, these strategies are designed to act for the short-term, meaning that they are meant to manage the conflict rather than resolve it. And they are usually implemented through the establishment of mechanisms and committees.

Efforts by ECOWAS

The two protocols by which ECOWAS has tried to resolve conflicts in the sub-region are firstly, the ECOWAS Protocol on Non-Aggression (1978) signed in Lagos and secondly, that Relating to Mutual Assistance on Defence (MAD) (1981), signed in Sierra Leone. The Protocol on Non-aggression provided essentially for the peaceful resolution of disputes between member states. The more elaborate protocol on Mutual Assistance on Defence (MAD) spelt out situations that would call for joint sub-regional action on external aggression, as well as interventions in inter-state and intra-state conflicts. MAD anticipated the conclusion of additional protocols, and provided organs for collective action.[5] These are the Authority of Heads of State and Government, Defence Council, Defence Committee, Allied Force of the Community, and the appointment in the ECOWAS secretariat of a deputy Executive Secretary for military matters.

With time, the above protocols were found to be quite limited in scope. The Non-Aggression Protocol for example, concerns itself with an emergency situation. It sees any armed threat against any member state as a threat or aggression against the community as a whole, and member-states therefore resolved to give mutual aid and assistance for defence against such armed threat or aggression. The protocol identified three possible situations which may require ECOWAS attention - these are internal armed conflict in a member-state, engineered and actively supported from without the community and likely to endanger peace and security of the entire community; an armed conflict between two or more member-states where the pacific procedures have proved ineffective; and an external armed threat or aggression.[6] By and large, the Protocol on Non-Aggression was criticized as a mere aspiration, as it failed to create an institutional mechanism for responding to such proscribed acts. It did not help to ally fears of instability within the sub-region.[7]

Basically, by adopting the Protocol Relating to Mutual Assistance on Defence (Defence Protocol) in 1981, ECOWAS leaders sought to address many of the limitations inherent in the 1978 Protocol on Non-Aggression. Unlike the Mutual Protocol, it applies as stated earlier, not only to conflicts between ECOWAS member states, but also to internal conflicts engineered and supported from outside and to aggressions perpetrated against an ECOWAS member state by non-ECOWAS countries. The Defence Protocol envisaged an elaborate security framework.

The enforcement arm of the Mutual Assistance on Defence framework is the Allied Armed Forces of the community (AAFC), a standby force comprised of national units earmarked from ECOWAS member states and available in case of 'any armed aggression'.[8] The protocol provides that the ECOWAS Authority would appoint a force commander to head AAFC. The procedure for engagement envisages that in a situation where an external armed threat or aggression is directed against an ECOWAS member, the written request of the besieged state triggers AAFC action. And in the case of a conflict between ECOWAS member states, the AAFC may be authorised to serve as an interposition force.[9] The AAFC is authorised to respond where an internal conflict in a member state of the community is actively maintained and sustained from outside. It is however, forbidden to intervene in a 'purely internal' conflict. This defence framework included decision-making and administrative structures. However, the MAD Protocol was never implemented for various reasons, the most plausible being a lack of political will by member countries of ECOWAS. It is widely believed that the Francophone states feared the overwhelming influence which Nigeria may exert within such a body, and whether indeed, such a mechanism would always be in the pursuit of common interests. It is also believed that the predilection in not taking the mechanism seriously was facilitated by the existence of a parallel security mechanism which is exclusively francophone in origin.

In view of the failure of past initiatives to really get off the drawing boards, by December 1999, the ECOWAS Summit agreed on a Protocol for the Establishment of a Mechanism for conflict Prevention, Management and Resolution, Peace and Security whose earlier draft had been endorsed by the Authority of ECOWAS Heads of State and Government in October 1998. This mechanism has a Council of Elders, as well as a Security and Mediation Council. The ten members of the mediation council are the foreign ministers of Benin, The Gambia, Guinea, Mali, Senegal, Côte d'Ivoire, Ghana, Liberia, Nigeria and Togo. This regional mechanism for conflict resolution provides a framework for regional intervention in political crisis in member states with ECOMOG as the adopted regional intervention force. This recommendation for ECOMOG to formerly become responsible for peacekeeping operations in West Africa was made by ECOWAS Foreign Ministers on 3 March 1998 in Yamoussoukro, Côte d'Ivoire. The Yamoussoukro decision reflected not only the reality of ECOMOG but served to recognise the dominant role of Nigeria although the decision provided for the broadening of the troop contributions and a rotating Force Commander, as opposed to predominantly Nigerian commanders.[10] Although, Nigeria shouldered the lion share of ECOMOG operations in Liberia and Sierra Leone, with a civilian government in power since 29 May 1999, it is going to be

70

rather difficult to get Nigeria to continue to shoulder such operations without a backlash from the civil society, unless member states and the international community augment the expenses.

However, this mechanism effectively replaced the ECOWAS Protocols Relating to Non-Aggression and Mutual Assistance on Defence (MAD). It is the highest decision-making body, but without prejudice, it delegated its powers in terms of Article 7 of the revised ECOWAS Treaty to the Mediation and Security Council. This is an innovative approach not very common with other regional bodies. The mediation and Security Council serves as the equivalent to the UN Security Council at sub-regional level and meets at Ambassadorial, Ministerial and at Heads of State levels. Acting on behalf of the authority of Heads of State it takes decisions on all issues relating to peace and security at the sub-region. For instance, the committee of Ambassadors of the nine elected member states of the council meet each month to review issues of peace and security. The Committee of members of Foreign Affairs, Internal Affairs and Security meet at least every three months 'to review the general political and security situations in the sub-region'. And the nine member Heads of State of the ECOWAS Mediation and Security Council meet at least twice a year and has the authority to make final decisions on the appropriate measures, policies and mandates to be taken with regard to situations under consideration with a two-thirds majority vote of the members present.[11]

The mediation and security council can authorise all forms of interventions, including the decision to deploy political and military missions, inform the UN and the OAU, now AU of its decisions, provide and review mandates and terms of reference, appoint force commanders, etc. The council can therefore, amongst others appoint a special representative as chief of a mission, appoint a force commander and deploy ECOMOG. Other components of the mechanism include the Defence and Security Commission, Executive Secretary, and the Council of Elders.

The Executive Secretary has the power to initiate fact-finding, mediation, facilitation, negotiations and reconciliation actions in the effective prevention and management of conflicts in the sub-region. The office of the Deputy Executive Secretary for Political Affairs, Defence and Security supervises the Departments of Political Affairs, Humanitarian Affairs, Defence and Security and the Observation and Monitoring centre. The Centre is the proposed hub of the Early Warning System that has four observation and monitoring zones within the sub-region – in Banjul (Gambia), Monrovia (Liberia), Ouagadougou (Burkina Faso) and Cotonou (Benin).

Overall, for ECOWAS, it can be said that the organization is growing in effectiveness and stature considering the roles it played in resolving the conflicts in Sierra Leone and Liberia. It requires the continued support of the Security Council of the UN and the international community in order to be able to achieve its objectives. The problems in West Africa transcend national borders, and therefore require a regional approach in devising and seeking solutions. ECOWAS has so far, tried to live up to the demands.

Accord de Non Agression et d'Assistance en matière de Défense (ANAD)

Seven Francophone West African countries signed this Accord in 1977 with the backing of the French government. It is considered as the security arm of the *Communauté de l'Afrique de l'Ouest* or the West African Economic Community (CEAO) with the addition of Togo. The impulse for its evolution was the same that prompted the creation of CEAO, that is the creation of a francophone security arrangement particularly after the border war between Burkina-Faso and Mali in 1974.[12] It was the first multilateral African mutual defence mechanism to be established, and, remarkably, considerable effort was made for its implementation. Over time, the Secretariat was made functional with other protocols and related instruments adopted. Thus, unlike the ECOWAS Protocol on Mutual Assistance and Defence, ANAD, had enough commitment for its implementation.[13]

Generally, ANAD demands of its members to abstain from all bellicose acts likely to engender conflict between them or with a third country and to refrain from the use of arms to settle their differences. Member states therefore, undertook to settle differences through dialogue, mediation, conciliation and arbitration; to respect the inviolability of boundaries inherited from colonisation, to maintain friendly and cordial relations in the border regions, and exchange security and police information for the purpose of maintaining peace.[14]

ECOWAS Ceasefire Monitoring Group (ECOMOG)

This regional security mechanism arose as a result of the rather intractable conflict going on in Liberia. Right from the onset, the international community stood akimbo, obviously leaving Liberians to their fate. Nigeria, a country which lays claim to regional hegemony, spearheaded the move for the formation of ECOMOG to intervene in the Liberian imbroglio. The decision to set up ECOMOG was taken at the first session of the standing committing on Liberia, held in Banjul, The Gambia from the 6th to 7th of August 1990. The meeting was chaired by The Gambia and attended by the Heads of State of The Gambia,

Sierra Leone, Guinea and Nigeria, while Mali and Togo sent high-powered delegations.[15]

Undoubtedly, Nigeria was a key actor in the formation of ECOMOG. Its power configuration in comparative terms to that of its neighbours in West Africa is substantial. With a population of over 120 million people, which is twice the combined population of the remaining fifteen countries in West Africa estimated at about 100 million, Nigeria is numerically massive. Also, Nigeria has a larger economy and market, and its military strength of about 100,000 fairly well equipped armed forces, compares quite favourably with an estimated 105,000 men for the rest of the sub-region, of which many of its national units lack a naval fleet and an Air force. The Country therefore, does indeed qualify as a regional hegemony in comparative terms. Perhaps, recognising its capacity, its leaders have consistently played major roles in economic, political and security affairs of the sub-region in spite of the cost implications. For instance, as at the 1999, ECOMOG operations in the Mano River Union had cost Nigeria about US $8 billion.

Though ECOMOG intervention in Liberia was carried out under very controversial circumstances, especially considering the reservations of the Franco-phone speaking countries, the legal and institutional framework of the ECOWAS Defence Protocol of May 1981, was seen as providing the basis for the operations in Liberia. Indeed, by construing the NPFL challenge to Samuel Doe's regime as an externally sponsored act of insurgency, Nigeria and other countries involved had little problem reconciling ECOMOG intervention and enforcement operation with the provisions of the protocol. Nigeria spearheaded this move through its proposal at the June 1990 Banjul summit for establishment of a standing committee on mediation in Liberia. This mediation committee consisted of Nigeria, Ghana, Gambia, Togo and Mali, otherwise referred to as the Committee of Five.

For ECOMOG, while it could not be denied that the Liberian civil war justified the invocation of Article 4b of the MAD Protocol, implementation of this had to be improvised. Not surprisingly, the initiative by the standing mediation committee alone to send troops into Liberia, and the composition of the troops from among its own members, not only raised legal issues, but forced the simmering anglophone-francophone divide into the open.

With the benefit of hindsight, though born under controversial circumstances, the ECOMOG initiative proved successful as a regional security mechanism. Though, Nigeria gained politically from this operation, it is difficult to see what economic gains it may have derived from its enormous sacrifice in men and materials in both Liberia and Sierra Leone. This perhaps, goes to buttress the point that its intervention under the auspices of ECOWAS and ECOMOG was largely benign. Indeed, it has been argued that in spite of its successes; ECOMOG appears to have created a 'post-triumphal depression', which makes it difficult for Nigeria to reap the benefits of her efforts. The view is therefore that Nigeria should learn from her mistakes in the ECOMOG operations, with respect to engaging in future operations.[16]

The Moratorium on Small Arms and Light Weapons

As part of the efforts at reducing the incidence of conflicts and insecurity in the sub-region, the moratorium on the importation, exportation and manufacture of light weapons was signed in Abuja on 31st October, 1998 during the 21st Summit of the ECOWAS Heads of State and Government. Its purpose was to halt the importation, exportation and manufacture of small arms in West Africa for an initial period of three years. The quantity of small weapons in circulation within the sub-region was estimated at about 15 million, which works out at one weapon for every 25 inhabitants, with about 80 per cent of the victims of small arms being civilians - mostly women and children.

The origin of the Moratorium could be traced to the November 1996 conference in Bamako, Mali on *Conflict Prevention, Disarmament and Development in West Africa*, jointly organized by the United Nations Institute for Disarmament Research (UNIDIR), and the United Nations Development Programme (UNDP). At this conference, representatives from 11 West African countries extensively discussed their individual security concerns, and the need for them to harmonize policies on arms control and conflict prevention in the region.[17] The interest generated by this conference and the follow-up actions by the representatives from the different countries led to the signing of the Moratorium at Abuja, two years later by the then 16 member states of ECOWAS.

When the foreign ministers in the sub-region met in Bamako, Mali, they defined the modalities for implementing the terms of the moratorium, specifically as embodied in the Programme of Co-ordination and Assistance on Security and Development (PCASED). To this end, the foreign ministers approved a plan of action in nine priority areas, namely: the development of a peace culture; creation of armed and security forces; increased controls at border posts, establishment of a regional light weapons database and register; collection and destruction of surplus arms and weapons in unauthorized possession; initiation of negotiations with arms producers and suppliers, harmonisation of relevant national legislation and administrative procedures; mobilization of resources for the activities set out under PCASED; the extension of the numbers of signatories to the moratorium.[18] The Moratorium,

74

commonly known as the West African Small Arms Moratorium entered into force on 1 November 1998, to be renewed every three years as mentioned. The Moratorium is not a legally-binding regime but rather an expression of shared political will. It is an innovative approach to peace-building and conflict-prevention. The Programme for Coordination and Assistance for Security and Development serves as the implementation mechanism for the Moratorium.[19]

Also, it has been earlier observed that in an attempt to enhance and invest greater legitimacy in the conflict resolving capacity of ECOWAS, the member states at their summit in Lome, Togo established the new Mechanism for Conflict prevention, Management, Resolution, Peace-keeping and Security. The structure of the new mechanism was eventually accepted by the ECOWAS Authority of Heads of State and Government in August 1998. The structure of the new mechanism comprises the Authority of Heads of State and Government; the Mediation and Security Council; the Defence and Security Commission; the Executive Secretary; the Council of Elders; and the Office of the Deputy Executive Secretary in charge of political affairs, defence and security.

However, a pertinent observation at this juncture is that it appears that efforts by ECOWAS at resolving conflicts have been basically confined to peacekeeping and peace-enforcement, as most of the mechanisms had largely been designed to be reactive rather than proactive. Still the conflicts continued in various parts of the sub-region, notably Liberia and Côte d'Ivoire. It is therefore, this intractability of conflicts in the sub-region, and the need to assemble long-term measures for seeking solutions that justified the emphasis on peace-building as a more sustainable solution.

For West Africa, peace initiatives and agreements never seem to be in short supply, Perhaps; it is time we re-focus our approach to seeking solutions by deciding to invest more in peace-building efforts. A process whereby conflict is avoided because there are nurtured structures available in society to contain the differences in society. This is obviously a proactive approach to the problem of conflict resolution in the sub-region.

In terms of being proactive, there is now a development within West Africa and indeed, in the African continent that is worth mentioning. It appears that West African leaders and ECOWAS member states have adopted some of the provisions of the Constitutive Act of the African Union[20] which came into being in June 2000, pertaining to conflicts and ways of addressing conflicts. The relevant sections in the Act include Articles 4(h)(j)(p) and Article 30. Under its principles, the Act in Article 4(h), stipulates 'the right of the Union to intervene in a Member State pursuant to a decision of the Assembly in respect of grave circumstances, namely, war crimes, genocide and crimes against humanity'. In

Article 4(j), it provides for 'the right of Member States to request intervention from the Union in order to restore peace and security'. Also, in Article 4(p), which is most significant, the Act stated its 'condemnation and rejection of unconstitutional changes of governments'. Following from this, in Article 30, it declares that 'Governments which shall come to power through unconstitutional means shall not be allowed to participate in the activities of the Union'. Considering Nigeria's and ECOWAS interventions in the crises in Guinea-Bissau and Sao Tome and Principe in 2004, and in Togo in 2005, after the unconstitutional assumption of office by Faure Gnassingbe at the demise of his father, President Gnassingbe Eyadema, it is clear that there is increasingly a new approach to conflict resolution in the sub-region. This is the adoption of the AU's principles on conflict resolution by ECOWAS member states. So far, this has worked under Nigeria's leadership in not only preventing the conflicts from escalating, but also in institutionalising certain practices, namely, that unconstitutional changes of governments including *coups d'états* are not only unacceptable, but will attract sanctions and possibly military interventions. In the case of Togo, Nigeria and ECOWAS initially imposed sanctions on the Faure Gnassingbe leadership before he wisely abdicated from office. Suffice it to observe, that the actions taken by ECOWAS in each case was geared towards resolving the disagreements and conflicts before they could escalate. To this extent, the strategy was pre-emptive and worked well at the level of diplomacy and third person intervention. However, were any of the parties to conflict recalcitrant and belligerent, and ECOWAS was forced to move on to the next level of resorting to peace enforcement, could it have been able to militarily persuade the belligerents? Apart from Nigeria which appears to have the military and financial muscle to do this, what about the capacities of the other member states and of ECOWAS itself? This is a problem that requires to be urgently addressed, especially in terms of mobilizing the resources necessary for a peace enforcement mission. As noted, the strategy is commendable when limited to the level of diplomacy and negotiations, and has a lot to offer in respect of its proactive, institutional and peace-building components.

What is evident from this analysis is that the likelihood of new conflict resolution mechanisms for the sub-region emerging cannot be discountenanced, while the existing ones will continue to be improved upon according to their practical relevance, a relevance that will be given more sustainability when considered from a regional perspective.

Notes

1. L. Reychler, 'The Art of Conflict Prevention: Theory and Practice', W. Bauwens and L. Reychler (eds.), *The Art of Conflict Prevention*, London, Brassey's, 1994, p.4.
2. Ibid.
3. G. Evans and J. Newnham, *The Dictionary of World Politics*, New York, Harvester Wheatsheaf, 1992, p.58.
4. S.A. Ochoche, 'Conflict Resolution and Prevention in West Africa: The Role of Education for Tolerance and a Culture of Peace, Paper presented at the Sub-regional Seminar on 'The Perspectives of Education for Tolerance as a Basis for Achieving a Culture of Peace in Africa, organised by the Nigerian National Commission for UNESCO, 15 - 17 August 2000, ECOWAS Secretariat, Abuja.
5. Olu Adeniji, *Mechanisms for Conflict Prevention in West Africa: Politics of Harmonisation*, Accord Occasional paper. 2/97.
6. O.A. Akinyeye, 'Regional Security and Integration: The ECOWAS Case', *Nigerian Journal of International Affairs*, Vol.19, No.2; See also Abass Bundu, 'The Experience and Lessons of Security Cooperation within ECOWAS: The Lessons of Liberia', lecture delivered at the High Level Workshop on Conflict Resolution and Crisis Prevention and Management and Confidence Building, organised by The UN Department of Disarmament Affairs, Yaounde, Cameroun, 17 - 21 June 1999, p.3.
7. Clement Adibe, *Managing Arms in Peace Process: Liberia*, United Nations Institute for Disarmament Research, 1996, p.15.
8. Eric G. Berman and Katie E. Sams, *Peacekeeping in Africa: Capabilities and Culpabilities, United Nations*, UNIDIR/ISS, Geneva, p.82.
9. Ibid.
10. Olu Adeniji, op cit.
11. Ibid.
12. Akinyeye, op cit. p.67.
13. *The West African Bulletin*, 'Farewell to Arms in Liberia', No.7, October 1999, p.30.
14. Celestine Bassey, 'Nigeria and Regional Security in the West African Sub-region: Lessons from Monrovia', *Nigerian Forum*, January - February, Vol.14, Nos.1 - 2, 1994, p.34.
15. *The West African Bulletin*, op cit, p.13.
16. Gani Joses Yoroms, 'ECOMOG and Nigeria's Foreign Policy', Bola A. Akinterinwa (ed.), *Nigeria's New Foreign Policy Thrust: Essays in Honour of Ambassador Oluyemi Adeniji*, Ibadan, Vantage Publishers.
17. Jacqueline Seck, *West Africa Small Arms Moratorium: High-Level Consultations on the Modalities for the Implementation of PCASED*, Geneva, UNIDIR/UNRCPDA, UNIDIR/ 2000/2, 2000, p.19.
18. *The West African Bulletin*, 1999, op cit.
19. Jacqueline Seck, 2000, p.3.
20. Organization of African Unity, *Constitutive Act of the African Union*, Lome-Togo, 12 June 2000.

8

Multilateral Organisations and Conflict Resolution in the Sub-region

Apart from the very significant role played by ECOWAS, the OAU (now AU) and the United Nations have been important partners in the effort at conflict resolution in the West Africa. The European Union was also very helpful in the Sierra Leonean peace process.

In the case of the UN, since its creation in 1945 it has been saddled with the all- important task of maintaining international peace and security. By this is meant that it is expected to act as the keeper of the peace. The drafters of its charter were more concerned then with inter-state rather than intra-state conflicts. This has therefore accounted for its inability to mediate effectively and judiciously in West African conflicts in the 1960, 1970 and also in the Nigerian civil war of 1967–1970. This is because many of the conflicts in Africa during these periods were mainly intra-state rather than inter-state conflicts in nature.

By late 1990s however, the UN evolved new mechanisms for dealing with intra-state conflicts within the international political system. The mechanism evolved revolved around the use of peacekeeping and peace-enforcement as key strategies. This made it possible for the organisation to contribute to the peace efforts in both the Liberian and Sierra Leonean conflicts of 1990–1997, and 1998–2001, respectively. However, it should be noted that the role the UN played in the conflicts was largely reactive rather than proactive. Its strategy was not meant to prevent the outbreak of conflict but rather to manage and at times.

In brief, the role of the UN in the resolution of conflicts in West Africa is basically what one could call *cordone-sanitaire*. In other words, it is both possible to keep and enforce the peace as long as the blue-helmets are on the ground. The drawback to this arrangement, prior to the introduction of PSOs was that the strategies only worked as a short-term measure.

In respect of the Liberian conflict (UNOMIL, 1993–1997), the UN role was mainly in response to the ECOWAS intervention, which had already taken place and consisted mainly in support of ECOMOG. A major mistake the UN made was not having intervened much earlier. The same belatedness could also be said of the (closely linked) conflict in Rwanda and in Sierra Leone where the deployment of UNOMSIL was delayed in 1998. UNOMSIL then comprised of only unarmed observers protected by ECOMOG, and followed later by a somewhat more strengthened UNAMSIL after a successful ECOMOG offensive to retake Freetown.[1]

For the OAU (now AU), its mechanisms for addressing conflicts in the continent of which West Africa was a major source of concern included the Commission of Mediation, Conciliation and Arbitration, the protocol of which was signed in 1964; the Ad hoc Commissions of the Heads of State and Government and council of ministers; and, the Mechanism of Conflict Prevention, Management, and Resolution established in 1993.[2] The Commission of Mediation, Conciliation and Arbitration was established under Article XIX of the organisation's charter.[3] Under this charter, 'member states pledged to settle all disputes among themselves by peaceful measures, and to this end, decided to establish a commission of mediation, conciliation and Arbitration'.[4] It is important to note however, that because the Protocol for the commission was not ready until 1964, and its bureau was not established until 1968, and because member states feared or were wary of the effects of judicial decisions on their sovereignty, and had a *stricto sensu* perception of international affairs, the commission was never effective.[5] The OAU had to adopt other measures such as ad hoc commissions; Good offices of OAU Heads of State and Government, summits and other such measures for conflict management and confidence building. These alternative ways were used to build confidence and mediate successfully in the border disputes between Ghana and Burkina Faso in 1964 and the dispute between Guinea and Cote D'Ivoire in 1967.[6]

The Mechanism of Conflict Prevention, Management, and Resolution (1993), was established at the Twenty-Ninth ordinary session of the OAU's Assembly of Heads of State and Government in Cairo, Egypt. This mechanism was designed as a catalyst to make the organisation more effective in the way it manages crises and conflicts in the continent. It had three main goals. First, to anticipate and prevent situations of potential conflict from developing into full-blown wars; Second, to undertake peace-making and peace-building efforts if full-blown conflicts should arise, and third, to carry out peace-making and peace-building activities in post-conflict situations. Even with its institutionalised approach and visibility- it was built around a central organ and the General Secretary, the mechanism proved ineffective in managing African conflicts like those that arose in Rwanda, Burundi, the Democratic Republic of Congo (DRC), and Comoros.[7]

Also, due to the importance it attached to conflict resolution in the continent, the OAU established an early warning system on conflict situations in Africa, based at the Conflict Management Center at the OAU headquarters in Addis Ababa.[8] This centre housed the Central Organ Conference Room, the Conflict Management and Peacekeeping Library and Documentation Center, the Situation and Control Room, the OAU Early Warning Network (EWARNET) and the Conflict Management Network (COMANET). However, the problem was not necessarily a lack of early warning signs, but rather the need to follow up effectively on early warning with prompt action.

The OAU also took steps to promote fundamental Human Rights as a confidence-building measure when it adopted the African Charter on Human and People's Rights in 1986.[9] Article 19 of the Charter asserts for example that, 'all People are equal, they shall enjoy the same respect and shall have the same rights. Nothing shall justify the domination of a people by another'. This was partly in recognition of the existence of apartheid in South Africa, and more generally recognition of the 'domination factor' as a recurrent source of conflict in the continent.

The conflict resolution mechanisms under the OAU/AU framework could be said to have served as the foundation for the emergence of a new continental security mechanism known as the Peace and Security Council (PSC). An organ under the AU framework. Nigerian President, Olusegun Obasanjo was selected as the first chairman of this council. The council was faced with the immediate task of finding solution to the crisis in Darfur region of Sudan in 2004. This was a crisis that began over disagreement between local black farmers and nomadic Sudanese Arabs over access to grazing land and water holes. The Sudanese government was accused of supporting the Janjaweed Arab militia in their military campaign, which some, especially the United States saw as ethnic cleansing against the black Sudanese population and black rebel groups fighting what they considered to be domination and marginalization by the Sudanese government. The AU sent in an observer force of 300 troops to enforce the ceasefire and maintain some peace, while talks continued on the possibility of increasing the force level as the situation dictated. However, apart from this initial effort at keeping the peace in the Darfur region in Sudan which is only a part of the larger Sudanese question, the problem of finding a long lasting solution to the conflict in Sudan remains, though efforts are still continuing in this direction. The difficulty in resolving the Sudanese conflict could be attributed to the complexity of issues involved, comprising issues of politicization of religion, access to power, marginalization, racism, colonial vestiges, resource allocation and more recently, purported ethnic cleansing and systematic rape of the black communities. Indeed, one is tempted to declare that if the AU can successfully resolve the Sudanese question, then almost every other conflict in Africa is resolvable. So far, the signs are good, as key parties to the conflict have agreed to abide by the comprehensive Peace Agreement signed in Nairobi, Kenya on January 9 2005. On July 9 2005, the revolutionary rebel leader of the Sudan Peoples Liberation Army (SPLA), John Garang, was sworn in as the First Vice-President of Sudan in a power-sharing arrangement in the spirit of the accords reached. However, the Darfur crisis remains a thorny issue for the new Sudan Unity Government.

Notes

1 Bjorn Moller, *Conflict Prevention and Peace-Building in Africa*, Copenhagen Peace Research Institute, working papers 28/2001.
2. S.A. Ochoche, 'Conflict Resolution and Prevention in West Africa', in Layi Erinosho et.al (eds), *Perspective on Education for Tolerance and Culture of Peace in Africa*, Abuja p.59. Nigeria National Commission for UNESCO, 2001.
3. T.A. Imobighe, 'Security in Sub-Saharan Africa', in J.Singh and Bernauer T. (eds.), *Security of Third World Countries*, United Nations Institute for Disarmament Research (UNIDIR), Partmouth Publishing Company, 1993, p.10.
4. Article 19 of the OAU Charter.
5. Thaddeus S. Akande, 'Confidence Building Mechanism for Crisis Management', in Chris Garuba, *Capacity Building for Crisis Management in Africa*, Lagos, 1998, p.99.
6. Ibid.
7. Monde Muyangwa and Margaret A. Vogt (eds), *An Assessment of the OAU Mechanism for Conflict Prevention, Management and Resolution, 1993 – 2000*, New York, International Peace Academy, November, 2000.
8. OAU, 'Resolving Conflicts', *OAU Conflict Management Bulletin*, Vol.1, No.6, October – November, 1996, p.7.
9. Thaddeaus Akande, 1998, op cit. p.100.

9

The Role of External Actors

A study of this nature cannot be complete without also examining the role or possible roles played by external actors in both the generation and resolution of conflicts in the region, especially in the Mano River Union. Some of these actors include the United States, France, mercenary organisations like Executive Outcomes and Sandline, and many NGOs, especially Humanitarian NGOs.

A major question that has often been raised is whether extra-African initiatives on conflict management are complementary to, competitive with or capable, in the long run, of supplanting existing autochthonous structures? It has been argued for instance, that the undertaking of extra initiatives conforms to the long-standing western tradition of seeking to play a prominent role in (re) shaping the destiny of Africans.[1] Often times, extra African interventions raise more questions than answers. However, there is a case to be made for external assistance or complementarity in seeking solutions to some of Africa's intractable conflicts.

External actors are usually necessary in providing support for the demobilization programme, training and reintegration of former combatants, funding advice and provision of neutral observers for post-war election purposes. Also, they are required for the training of judges, police and parliamentarians, support for an independent media; and equally play an important role in helping former armed rebels to become acceptable political players.

Unlike in the 1970s when foreign military interventions were rampant in Africa, the 1990s witnessed a much-reduced interest in African conflicts, rather like half-hearted efforts at complementary regional conflict resolution efforts. This is probably as a result of the end of cold war politics. Also, a justification of this maybe as a result of the fact that attention by extra-continental powers was riveted on the geo-strategically explosive situations in the Persian Gulf and the Balkans. However, it suffices to note that there was what may be regarded as 'Afro-pessimism' amongst Africa's development partners, a situation in which donors were simply tired of African problems, and therefore diverted attention away from Africa. In this case, the areas where assistance was required from external partners included logistics, command and control, communications, capacity building and funding.[2]

As a way of responding to the conflicts in West Africa and to future conflicts that may arise, the United States did put forward the idea of an African Crisis Response Force, later African Crisis Response Initiative (ACRI). The initial expectation was that of establishing a standing force of about 10,000 troops with a view to being in a position to intervene rapidly in conflict situations with grave humanitarian crisis. After almost a year of extensive consultations by the US with its allies (Britain, France, Italy, Canada, Brazil, the Netherlands, Germany and Japan) and with African Governments as well as with the UN and the OAU, this initial plan was abandoned and instead, an 'inter-operable peace-keeping capability offering training to African States interested in enhancing their peace-keeping capacity' was established.[3] Even then, this initiative was just not available to all willing states, but only to those with (sic) 'stable democratic countries that can work together to maintain peace on the continent'. Nigeria in particular, had problems with this initiative, as it was then under military rule, though it was spearheading the ECOWAS regional force. Some African States that participated in this programme, included Senegal, Uganda, Malawi Mali and Ghana. But all this changed with Nigeria's successful transition to democratic governance. The US government is presently more predisposed to collaborating with Nigeria. In 2003, it donated six naval vessels to the Nigerian Navy to enhance its capacity in patrolling the coastal waters as a way of checking the nefarious activities of pirates. The pirates who were sabotaging oil pipelines and abducting oil workers for a ransom had caused widespread insecurity in the Niger Delta, and disrupted oil production activities.

On the other hand, the rivalry between the United States and France, manifested in the establishment of France's Reinforcement of African Capacity for Peace-keeping (RECAMP), launched in January 1998. Buoyed up by the success of its Inter-African Stabilisation Mission to Bangui (MISAB) in 1997, this initiative was launched as an exclusively inter-African peacekeeping force.[4] However, let us reiterate the fact, that when indeed, urgent assistance was needed from extra Africa powers during the Liberian war, none was forthcoming from both countries. Therefore, in a sense, it was in the interest of

83

the United States and France not to contribute directly, but rather indirectly through proxy, without having to send in their own troops.

Therefore, in terms of foreign policy priority and even strategic rating, neither Liberia nor even the West African sub-region qualified for immediate assistance in their period of crisis.[5] Indeed, the over-all decline in the total number of French troops in Africa in subsequent years indicated this line of policy by western governments. In fact, French Africa policy has a reputation for being unaffected by its domestic opinion since this policy is treated as *chasse garde*, an exclusive preserve, of the President. France would not have been expected to lend an enthusiastic support to ECOMOG since its principal ally in the sub-region, Côte d'Ivoire, as well as Burkina Faso were among the prime backers of Charles Taylor's insurgency in Liberia.

Nevertheless, we need to recognize the contributions of certain NGOs in alleviating the humanitarian crisis generated by the civil wars in the Mano River Union. For example, French NGOs particularly, *Médecins Sans Frontiers* (MSF), among others, and indeed the French Government through its erstwhile Secretary of State for Humanitarian Affairs, Bernard Kouchner, played significant roles in alleviating the sufferings of victims of the Liberia crisis in the 1990s.

In as much as extra African initiatives may be due to certain national interests of the initiating countries, they do sometimes reflect a genuine concern for the humanitarian tragedies that have overwhelmed an alarming number of states in Africa. As recent events in Liberia, Sierra Leone and Côte d'Ivoire revealed, the international community is slowly but surely retreating from being entangled in the intra-state conflicts occurring with alacrity in the West African sub-region. The onus therefore lies with member states of the sub-region to devise means of strengthening, and possibly harmonizing existing conflict resolution mechanisms with a view to having a more coordinated and effective framework.

Notes

1. Emeka Nwokedi, 'Extra-African Conflict Management Initiatives and African Security'.Paper read at the Regional Conference on *The Management of African Security in the 21ˢᵗ Century*, Nigerian Institute of International Affairs, Lagos, 23 – 24 June, 1999, p.3.
2. J Adisa, 'The Politics of Regional Military Cooperation: The Case of ECOMOG',Vogt M. A. (ed), *The Liberian Crisis and ECOMOG: A Bold Attempt at Regional Peacekeeping*, Lagos, Gabumo Publishing Co., 1992. See also, M.A. Vogt and L.S. Aminu (eds), *Peace-keeping as a Security Strategy in Africa: Chad and Liberia as Case Studies*, 2 vols., Enugu, Fourth Dimension Publishing Co., 1996.

3. Emeka Nwokedi, 1999, op cit. p.6.
4. Ibid, p.7.
5. Emeka Nwokedi, 'Resources and International Support for Conflict ManagementMechanisms in West Africa', Olu Adeniji (ed), *Report of the Workshop on Conflict Management Mechanism in West Africa*, African Strategic and Peace Research Group (AFSTRAG), 1997, P.77.
6. Ibid, p.78.

10

The Imperative for Peace-Building

The histories and lessons from the conflicts in the Mano River Union and in fact, the West African sub-region have strengthened the position and indeed, argument that peace-building is a better alternative for ensuring that conflicts do not arise or resurge in the first instance. As a long-lasting strategy to the maintenance of stability, peace building should be inbuilt into any serious conflict resolution framework with a view to ensuring that the people are made part and parcel of the peace design.

It appears that the UN should be given pride of place, in terms of the origin and operationalisation of post-conflict peace building processes. In fact, it was ONUSAL, the UN Observer Group to El-Salvator, with its human rights verification mandate and its emphasis on judicial, military and police reform, that undertook a role unprecedented in UN history, by moving its peace-keeping activities further into the areas of peace-building and democratisation.[1]

United Nations Peace Support Operations (PSOs), from which the peace-building repertoire emerged, have been from experience highly complex operations. PSOs usually involve a bewildering array of actors from a variety of backgrounds with different levels of experience, not to mention motivations, and engaging in what is intrinsically a deeply politicised and resource-challenged process.[2] Peace-building as a process equally involves a multiplicity of actors or agencies. These include government departments, national and international relief and development actors, non-governmental organizations, private sector companies, international financial institutions and regional organizations. Therefore, part of this complexity is in terms of being able to coordinate this vast but important array of actors.

The UN Secretary-General, Boutros Boutros Ghali in 1992, had described the main tasks of post-settlement peacebuilding as:

Disarming the previously warring parties and restoration of order, the custody and possible destruction of weapons, repatriating refugees, advisory and training support for security personnel, monitoring elections, advancing efforts to protect human rights, reforming or strengthening governmental institutions and promoting formal and informal processes of political participation.[3]

Usually, military activities under PSOs are designed to conclude conflicts by conciliation among competing parties, rather than a short-term and superficial termination of the conflict by force. Experience has shown that in trying to reconcile conflicting parties after a war, all too frequently sufficient effort and resources necessary for this reconciliation are lacking. Oftentimes, the conditions for assisting in the peace-building efforts are unacceptable to the indigenous population. It is therefore, the inability to allocate resources to the post conflict peacebuilding phase, to oversee the return of refugees, to reform the security sector, and to assist in the establishment of a workable form of government that causes the majority of operations to end in stalemate from which the engaged military and civilian agencies cannot easily disengage.[4]

It is also very important not to forget the local constituency in designing any peace-building process. For instance, the ultimate success of any peace accord is to be found in the extent to which its local constituents perceive the benefits of abiding by that agreement. There is therefore, a need for marketing support for any peace settlement. A marketing perspective guides the analyst to explore the feasibility of promoting domestic support for an accord, by appealing to targeted groups on the basis of the most attractive attributes of peace.[5] Responsibility and ownership of the peace-building projects should therefore be given to the locals as soon as it is practicable. Also, mechanisms for continuous funding, of which the locals should also have access need to be developed so that projects do not grind to a halt once international agents of peace-building leave a post-conflict environment.

Peace-building as a strategy for enthroning peace, is therefore a proactive approach, as opposed to the rather reactive nature of previous conflict resolution mechanisms in West Africa. The Mechanism for Conflict Prevention, Management and Resolution, Peace and Security however, came close to approximating both a peacekeeping and a peace-building approach.

At the sub-regional level, both ECOWAS and ANAD have very important roles to play in peace building. ECOWAS must at this period avoid at all costs the mistakes of the past, which led to the recrudescence of conflicts in places where it had helped to broker peace. It should be flexible and ensure that its mandate during conflict resolution includes not only peacekeeping and peace-enforcement but also peace-building. The implication of this is that peace-building will necessarily compel ECOWAS to ensure that the political and socio-economic factors, which led to the outbreak of hostilities in the first instance, would have been addressed before it disengages itself from any conflict area.

Since the basic factors responsible for intra-state conflicts in West Africa are largely political, economic and social in origin, efforts should be made by ECOWAS to monitor post-conflict environments through the use of monitors, so that whichever 'new' government has been put in place by the people, stays loyal to the spirit and letter of the peace agreements.

For the West African sub-region, it is absolutely important for peace to reign in the sub-region, and that the unnatural colonial inherited divide between the Francophone and Anglophone countries be bridged positively. The importance of making English and French languages prime languages for all in this sub-region cannot be overemphasized. Ideally, these languages should be made compulsory for all students from the primary to the secondary levels of education so that even if one cannot speak either of these fluently, one could at least understand when spoken to. This will help immensely in ensuring that the right level of communication is established amongst the peoples of the sub-region. ECOWAS could make legislation to this effect and enforce this by monitoring its implementation at the level of the national governments. This can only contribute to empowering those engaged in the peace-building process in the sub-region.

Truth commissions have in recent times become fashionable as peace-building instruments. However, it appears that there is the absolute necessary to invest Truth and Reconciliation Commissions with the necessary powers with which they can function more effectively. The Sierra Leonean example is a case in point. The *raison d'être* for Truth Commissions is to help heal the scars of the wars; make these wars better understood; help the parties to the conflict in understanding themselves better and ultimately help in not only understanding the peace-building measures put in place but also in preventing a resurgence of the conflict. Such a commission should therefore be invested with the powers to arrest and prosecute. However, a similar or complementary body can also do this. In this way, those wronged during the war, will have little reason for picking up their arms once again.

The imperative for peace building has also been justified by the moratorium on exportation, importation and manufacture of light weapons in West Africa. Though laudable, there is abundant evidence that many countries have not taken this seriously as wars of both medium to high intensity still continue in the sub-region indicating that light weapons are still very much in circulation and in use.

Related to the whole issue of building peace in West Africa, is the economic dimension of these conflicts, especially the fact that these wars have been largely funded by proceeds from the sale of natural resources found in the conflict areas. The bloody Sierra Leone war was believed to have lasted so long as it did, because of the funding proceeds from the sale of illegal diamonds. Only recently, probably as a result of the success of the peace process in Sierra Leone, the UN Security Council agreed to end the ban on the export of 'blood diamonds' from Sierra Leone. This ban has been in effect since 2000 to prevent rebels of the RUF from using diamonds to pay for weapons. However, the ban on diamond exports from Liberia imposed because of its government's alleged links to the RUF remains in place. This is in tandem with the Kimberley Process, developed by the diamond industry, human rights groups and dozens of governments, aimed at stifling the trade in illicit diamonds to fund wars in Africa. The certification process is intended to track each diamond from the mine to the jeweller's window, effectively blocking the trade in illicit and blood diamonds[6]. In terms of peace-building efforts, this approach at stifling the source(s) of funding for these deadly wars has been effective. It has implications for the efforts at rehabilitating and stopping the use of child soldiers in these wars. It also has implications for the moratorium on small arms and light weapons.

There is however, little doubt that the Mano River Union countries seem mired in continuing conflict if something as enduring as regional peace-building initiatives involving all these countries and their neighbours are not given the attention that is necessary. Although, elections were successfully held in Sierra Leone, fighting in Liberia between Taylor's forces and the LURD rebels continued with Monrovia under siege as at June 2003. This type of development in Liberia is provoked fears that a spill-over effect might threaten not only Sierra Leone's hard won and still fragile stability, but also contain seeds of further destabilization in Côte d'Ivoire, Guinea, Burkina Faso and Guinea Bissau. It has been observed, and rightly too that stability will be difficult to achieve in the MRU unless Liberia is at peace. This is because deposed leader, Charles Taylor, had and still has supporters in Côte d'Ivoire; LURD still has its own supporters in Liberia, and even in Guinea. So what we have is that any major military activity inside Liberia will inevitably have repercussions in Côte d'Ivoire, Guinea and of course Sierra Leone.

However, what may be considered a positive development on the Liberian war is the signing of an Agreement in June 2003 in Accra, Ghana by eleven parties to the conflict concerning a ceasefire, but on the basis that Charles Taylor ceases to be the President. Mercifully, Charles Taylor was convinced of the necessity for him to abdicate his Presidency as a desideratum for stability in Liberia by Nigeria and other ECOWAS countries. Nigeria offered Taylor and his family political asylum, which he accepted and is presently living in Calabar, a coastal town in the Southern part of Nigeria. It is however, heartening to observe that ECOWAS, and indeed, the AU, are now aware of the need to seek regional peace not necessarily through military campaigns, but also through political negotiations that involve power-sharing arrangements, resource allocation and reconciliation measures. It has been observed for instance, that of the three measures – disarmament, demobilization and reconciliation – reconciliation is the most difficult to attain because it has both psychological and economic dimensions.

For stability to be achieved in West Africa, and for peace and security to be long lasting, measures need to be initiated and implemented in a coordinated manner suitable for the sub-region as a 'security complex'. In identifying the threats in the sub-region, this has to be done, not just in terms of the military implications and impact, but also in terms of ensuring human security for the greatest number of ECOWAS citizens. Geographical contiguity, historical, political and cultural affinities, and the common goal of economic integration to enhance development in the sub-region clearly define the 'security complex' of this area as espoused by Barry Buzan[7]. It therefore, appears that the ECOWAS member states have little option but to cooperate comprehensively towards attaining their political, economic and social goals. This cooperation has even become more imperative in this age of competitive industrialisation and globalisation, in which weak countries are at a great disadvantage. From this viewpoint, peace-building before, during and after conflicts should therefore be a cardinal development strategy of ECOWAS and its member states in its bid to grow the economy and enhance human security in the sub-region.

In promoting peacebuilding, the teaching of peace education and tolerance at all strata of society is imperative. Local and international NGOs, political parties, the media, professional associations and national governments must all work together nationally and regionally to promote peace initiatives and good governance.

Notes

1. Robin Hay, *Peace-building During Peace Support Operation: A Survey and Analysis of Recent Mission* Canada, Department of Foreign Affairs and International Trade, 1999, p.5.
2. Ibid, p.4. Since 1989, over twenty-six missions have been launched, bearing little resemblance to earlier UN operations; they contain predominantly civilian elements with far more complex mandates.

3. Johan Galtung, 'Cultural Violence', *Journal of Peace Research*, Vol.27, No.3, 1981, pp.291-305.
4. Philip Wilkinson, 'Sharpening the Weapons of Peace: Peace Support Operations and Complex Emergencies', *Peacekeeping and Conflict Resolution*, 1998, p.69.
5. Walter Isard, 'Formative and Early Years of the Peace Science Society (International)', *Conflict Management and Peace Science*, Vol.18, No.1, 2000, p.98.
6. M. Bendi, UN lifts ban on 'blood Diamonds', Internet site: http//www.mbendi.co.za/a_sndmsg/news-view.asp?¹=497a5. Visited Agust 2004
7. Barry Buzan, *People, States and Fear: The National Security Problem in International Relations*, Sussex, Wheatsheaf Books Ltd., 1983, p.106

11

Conclusion

> The process of peace building is much more difficult in reality than its description portrays. This is because peace has eluded the numerous conflicts in Africa, and where it has been brokered it is usually of a fragile nature.[1]

The above statement clearly indicates the difficulty inherent in embarking on any peace-building project in the African continent. However, the consolation is that this cannot be done by any one single country or actor but by a combination of actors, countries, organisations and individuals. It has come to a stage in West Africa, where peace education should become very relevant as a compulsory subject in the curricula. This is because of the enormous cost in human lives and loss of property, which wars have brought upon the peoples of West Africa. Civil wars and inter-state conflicts have largely reduced millions of dollars of development invested in Liberia, Sierra Leone, and Côte d'Ivoire over the last twenty-five years to rubbles .

Political succession and problems associated with bad governance have often led to conflicts in the sub-region as witnessed in the Mano River Union. In fact, Adekeye Adebayo[2] was to attribute the conflicts in Liberia, Sierra Leone and Guinea-Bissau to personalized autocratic rule. In other words, good governance as part of the repertoire of peace-building must be embraced and nourished in the sub-region as a basis for peace and stability.

It is good that the necessity for good governance was engrained in the New Partnership for Africa's Development (NEPAD) document, which sought to set standards through the Peer Review Mechanism to hold African leaders accountable for their actions through their own voluntary role as watch-dogs over economic and political developments in their various countries. It therefore goes without saying, that the future has no place for bad leaders and bad governance and indeed, autocratic rule, which generates dynamics most unsuitable for peace and stability. This is not to say that democracy on its own is the perfect panacea to problems associated with governance. Democracy also inherently produces its own conflicts (as does development).[3] For instance, in Africa democracy has been known to throw up otherwise nascent or dormant ethnic nationalism, which in response to the freedom provided by a democratic environment to make demands for economic restitution or self-determination on the fragile post-colonial states.

However, considering the dovetailing nature of the conflicts in the Mano River Union, countries in this Union have very little option but to embrace good governance and support a regional framework to building peace in the area. This regional level of action is more effective for managing problems of ethnic groups and nations' 'straddling borders', sharing resources, as well as characterised by the movements of migrants, refugees and transborder crime. For the MRU, the problem of what may be regarded as the 'exportation of conflicts' obviously requires a regional approach to addressing this dangerous dimension.

It has been rightly observed that sustainable and appropriate rebuilding after violent conflict is a prerequisite for the prevention of future conflicts.[4] However, what is also clear from the experiences of peace-building is that local contexts differ in their requirements regarding how policy makers and other actors should plan, coordinate and implement their assistance. Whereas peace-building efforts in Sierra Leone could be said to be a success, in Liberia it was a failure. A failure in the sense, that Liberia succumbed to resurgence of their conflict. Whereas the peace process in Sierra Leone was reasonably transparent, in Liberia, the government of Charles Taylor refused to honour agreements reached by the warring parties. This created room for suspicious, doubts, fears and ultimately a reversal and recourse to the only way available to those marginalized and brutalized – retreat to the bush paths.

Since reconciliation is an incremental process, a long-term perspective is important. Hence, endurance is also important both for donors, policy makers, the civil society and the parties that are in conflict. Tradeoffs typically occur in the short-run, such as striking a balance between justice and reconciliation. Further efforts to promote reconciliation and democratisation in countries affected by serious conflicts make new demands on the international community.[5]

In terms of short and long-term measures which may be helpful in resolving the conflicts in the Mano River Union, this contribution to the already significant literature on conflicts and peace-building in West Africa, maintain that a regional peace-building approach to addressing these conflicts is a more sustainable way of ensuring the stability of the West African sub-region.

In furtherance of this position therefore, the following should be uppermost in the minds of all, but especially those involved in the peace-building process in West Africa:

- In the first instance, a lot has been said about the need for good governance. There is a need to make the political leaders and those who aspire to leadership positions to realise that their first priority is to improve the welfare of their peoples, and not themselves, relatives and cronies.

- There is also the imperative for unified conflict resolution mechanism in West Africa. This is important in order to overcome the problems created by the existence of the dual mechanisms and the concomitant Anglophone/francophone rivalry. Efforts should be made to see how the new ECOWAS conflict resolution mechanism and ANAD could be integrated for more effectiveness in addressing conflicts within the sub-region. This should be done bearing in mind the other efforts at containing conflicts within the ambit of the African Union (AU), and the New Partnership for Africa's Development (NEPAD) frameworks.

- For achieving success in peace building programmes, contextual understanding of each case is necessary for effective intervention. In principle, the complexity and contradictions inherent in the historical and social processes of the particular situation should be taken into account. The locals must be made part and parcel of the implementation process; otherwise 'spoilers' will jeopardise the peace-building efforts. The peace-building process in Sierra Leone, which turned out to be a success story, is a case in point.

However, the Liberian case teaches us how not to broker peace without leaving an all embracing or broad political platform for all if not most of the warring factions in the post conflict situation. This is because the resurgence in Liberia's civil war could partly be explained by the nature of the post-conflict political architecture which made the winner of the presidential elections wield disproportionate powers to the detriment of the other actors who invariably had little say in the political life of the country after the hostilities. Because it was a post-conflict situation, what should have been devised was a system that allowed for the sharing of powers amongst the key actors, as a way of not only having their interests protected, but also their fears dispelled. This would logically have enhanced the reintegration process. In short, whereas post-conflict situations call for strengthening public authority and making it legitimate in the eyes of all the citizens, nonetheless, for the sake of sustainable peace and stability, constitutive politics should at this period pave the way for more effective distributive politics.

Aside from the institution of conflict resolution mechanisms with regard to the Mano River Union, a key factor in enthroning peace and stability in the region lay in resolving the crisis in Liberia, both with respect to the LURD insurgency and the democratisation process within the Mano River Union. The character of conflicts within the MRU require that whilst international sanctions and pressure on the Taylor government had their uses, it is equally important to make political leaders understand why proper representation and reintegration, democratisation and human rights issues are important factors for stability in any region. Desisting from subterranean support to rebel activities on the part of the leaders of the MRU can only help in reducing the cycle of instability in the region.

The lessons from the conflicts in the MRU also show that there is a need for early international attention and prompt action by the United Nations, through the Security Council. The lack of attention to the Liberian war during the 1990s, and Nigeria's largely humanitarian intervention clearly brings this point into sharp relief. For the future, there should be a quick agreement to an appropriate, clearly defined and robust mandate, in consonance with regional conflict resolution mechanisms for any peacekeeping force backed by adequate resources. All UN efforts must be integrated within this peacekeeping mission, as peacekeepers are more successful when they work alongside human rights specialists, development experts and the humanitarian community. The experience from the Sierra Leone peacekeeping is a good example of this synergy of efforts.

Security sector reform, reform of judicial and penal systems, and building respect for human rights are all equally important in peace-building in the MRU. Security sector reform, for example, should get underway, while the protective umbrella of the UN peacekeeping operations remains. The issue of impunity during wars must be addressed as in the case of Sierra Leone through the use of the Special Court and the Truth and Reconciliation Commission. This not only helps to get the truth into the open, but also helps heal wounds and indeed, may bring justice to some. For the Nigerian case, addressing impunity concerning the manipulation of votes by the political parties, electoral bodies and the security agencies should be of top priority. This is because Nigeria's fragile democracy stands to be truncated if this practice is not checked. The result can only be violence and instability with grave implications for the country and the sub-region.

It has been observed that it is difficult to say with any certainty whether peacekeeping is more expensive than peace-building and vice versa. The issue of cost logically depends on the particular nature of the conflict and the dynamics of the situation. However, adequate funding must be sourced *ab initio* for post-conflict peace-building initiatives otherwise it may run into problems. In Sierra Leone for example, UNAMSIL gulped $700 million a year, yet it was difficult to find even $13 million for the reintegration efforts.[6] Multilateral, bilateral and other sources of funding are needed to ensure adequate resources for peace-building activities.

Disarmament, Demobilisation and Reintegration (DDR) should also be built into peace agreements and follow-up programmes for mopping up stray weapons and ammunition put in place. Experience from Sierra Leone indicates that this is necessary to prevent possible sporadic violence which may result from the availability of these stray weapons in a post-conflict environment. From a regional perspective, the continuing flow of small arms within West Africa threatens its stability. To this extent, the moratorium on small arms should be reinforced and an arms control mechanism put in place

Peace-building efforts should have special provisions for children, girls and women who oftentimes suffer disproportionately during wars. Peacekeeping mandates should include the special protection and assistance for the needs of girls and women. Not necessarily in terms of gender mainstreaming, but in the institutionalised responses to endemic gender-based violence and sexual exploitation. In this wise, special attention should be paid to gender issues in justice and reconciliation.

Refugee flows can indeed, be an indicator of trouble or conflict to come. Therefore, there is an urgent need to address the refugee problem as part and parcel of the peace-building efforts in the sub-region. This is because it has security implications for many of the countries, especially those that invariably act as host communities. Usually, what they face is a circumstance, not of their own making, but with implications for the own stability. Guinea is a case in point.

Finally, the present character of the international political and economic environments compel each state to conceive of its security and stability as part and parcel of those of its neighbours and the international community. With the increasing enmeshment of peoples, markets and ideas; and with the obliteration of time and boundaries as constants in human relationships, conflicts can more easily be resolved; while ironically it could also be more easily ignited and exported. This is why it is absolutely imperative that we embrace consistent peace-building as part and parcel of the overall security architecture, not only in the West African sub-region but also at the global level. It appears that West Africa is gradually emerging from the long and painful period of bloody conflicts, as a result of the efforts being made by ECOWAS, the UN, partners and other multilateral bodies. The challenge remains to ensure that peace-building measures are seen to logical conclusion. To this extent, global support for regional conflict resolution efforts as we have seen in West Africa need to be further strengthened for the sake of humanity.

Notes

1. R.A. Akindele and O.D. Oche, 'The United Nations and African Security: Peace-keeping, Peace-enforcement and Post-conflict Peace-building', paper presented at the Regional Conference on the Management of African Security in the 21ˢᵗ Century, Nigerian Institute of International Affairs (NIIA), Lagos, June 23 – 24, 1999, p.17.
2. Joe Wylie's Review of Adekeye Adebajo, *Building Peace in West Africa: A Review*, IPA, Internet site: http://www.copla.org/wylieandnyenpan.htm.Visited August 2004.
3. Jean Herskovits (1998), *Africans Solving African Problems: Militaries, Democracies, and Security in West and Southern Africa*, Report of a Conference on sub-Saharan Africa Security Project, New York.
4. Summary Report of Bergen Seminar on Development 2000, *After War: Reconciliation and Democratisation in Divided Societies – Lessons Learned*, CMI Conference Report, Chr. Michelsen Institute, 2000.
5. Ibid. p.3.
6. UK Mission to the United Nations, Security Council Workshop on the Mano River Union, Internet site: http://www.ukun.org/scp2002/xq/asp/sarticleType7/Article-ID.469/qx/articles-show.htm. Visited August 2004.

Bibliography

Abdullah, Ibrahim, 2004, *Between Democracy and Terror: The Sierra Leone Civil War*, Dakar: CODESRIA

Adeniji, O., 1997, *Mechanisms for Conflict Prevention in West Africa: Politics of Harmonisation*, Accord Occasional paper, 2/97.

Adeniji, O., ed., 1997, *Report of the Workshop on Conflict Management Mechanism in West Africa*, African Strategic and Peace Research Group (AFSTRAG).

Adetula, V., 1982, 'ECOWAS and the Liberian Crisis: An Approach in Conflict Management', *Nigerian Forum*, Vol.12, Nos.9-12, September-December.

Adibe, C., 1996, *Managing Arms in Peace Process: Liberia*, United Nations Institute for Disarmament Research.

Africa Research Bulletin, 1998,'Uprising in Guinea Bissau', Vol.35, No.6, 1-30 June.

Africa, South of the Sahara, 1999.

Agbu, O., 2004, *Ethnic Militias and the Threat to Democracy in Post-Transition Nigeria*, Research Report no. 127, Uppsala, Nordiska Afrikanstitutet.

Agbu, O., 2000, 'Democratization of Education for Refugees and Displaced Persons', Layi Erinosho et al. (eds.), *Perspectives on Education For Tolerance and a Culture of Peace in Africa*, Abuja, Federal Ministry of Education, Nigerian National Commission for UNESCO.

Agbu, O., 2000, 'Human Rights Implications of African Conflitcs', *African Journal of Political Science*, Vol.5, No.1, June.

Agbu, O., 2004, 'Re-inventing Federalism in Post-Transition Nigeria: Problems and Prospects', *Africa Development*, Vol. XXIX, No.2.

Agbu, O., 2002,'Sub-regional Dynamics of the Resurgent Conflicts in Liberia', *Nigerian Forum*, Vol.23, Nos. 9-10.

Akindele, R.A and Oche, O.D., 1999, 'The United Nations and African Security: Peace-keeping, Peace-enforcement and Post-conflict Peace-building', Being paper presented at the Regional Conference on the Management of African Security in the 21st Century, Nigerian Institute of International Affairs (NIIA), Lagos, June 23 – 24.

Akintayo, O. and Agbu, J-Frances, 2002, 'Psychological Implications of Ethno-Religious Conflicts in Nigeria', *Nigerian Forum*, July/August.

Akinterinwa, A. Bola, 2004, *Nigeria's New Foreign Policy Thrust: Essays in Honour of Ambassador Oluyemi Adeniji*, Ibadan: Vantage Publishers.

Akinyeye, O.A, 1993, 'Regional Security and Integration: The ECOWAS Case', *Nigerian Journal of International Affairs*, Vol.19, No.2.

Amnesty International, 1999, SIERRA LEONE: Recommendations to the International Contact Group on Sierra Leone, New York, April 19.

Anan, Kofi, 1997, *Reform Announcement*, UN 16 July, Part 2.

Ayissi, A. and Paulton, R., eds., 2000, *Bound to Cooperate*: Conflict, Peace and People in Sierra Leone, Geneva: UNIDIR.

Barnes, C. & Polzer, T., 2000, *Sierra Leone Peace Process: Learning from the Past to Address Current Challenges*, An Expert Seminar Report, London, 27 September.

Basic Papers, 1997, *Africa: The Challenge of Light Weapons Destruction during Peacekeeping Operations*, Basic Publications, No.23, December.

Bassey, C., 1994, 'Nigeria and Regional Security in the West African Sub-Region: Lessons from Monrovia', *Nigerian Forum*, Vol.14, Nos.1 & 2, , January-February.

Berdal, Mats R., 1996, 'Disarmament and Demobilization After Civil Wars: Arms, Soldiers and the Termination of Armed Conflicts', London International Institute for Strategic Studies, Adelphi paper 303.

Bergen, Summary Report of Seminar on Development 2000, 'After War: Reconciliation and Democratisation in Divided Societies – Lessons Learned, CMI Conference Report, Chr. Michelsen Institute.

Berman, Eric G. and Sams, Katie E., 2000, *Peacekeeping in Africa: Capabilities and Culpabilities*, Geneva: UNIDIR.

Best, Shadrack G., 1998, 'The Underdeveloped State of Peace and Conflict Studies in Africa', *African Peace Review*, Vol.2, No.1, April.

Blell, Joe C., 1999, 'Nigeria-Sierra Leone bilateral relations as well as current developments in Sierra Leone', Ambassadorial Forum, Nigerian Institute of International Affairs, Lagos, June.

Boas, M., 2001, 'Liberia and Sierra Leone – dead ringers? The logic of neopatrimonial rule', *Third World Quarterly*, Vol.22, No.5.

Boutros-Ghali, Boutros, 1992, *An Agenda for Peace*, New York, United Nations.

Boutros-Ghali, Boutros, 1995, 'An Agenda for Peace: 'Preventive Diplomacy', Peace-Making and Peacekeeping', Stockholm International Peace Research Institute Yearbook, Oxford: Oxford University Press.

Bratton, M. and Van de Walle, N., 1998, 'Neopatrimonial Regimes and Political Transitions in Africa', P. Lewis (ed.), *Africa: the Dilemmas of Development and Change*, Boulder Co.: Westview.

Bundu, A., 1999, 'The Experience and Lessons of Security Cooperation within ECOWAS: The Lessons of Liberia', lecture delivered at the High Level Workshop on Conflict Resolution and Crisis Prevention and Management and Confidence Building, organised by The UN Department of Disarmament Affairs, Yaounde, Cameroon, 17 - 21 June.

Burton John, 1987, *World Society*, Lanham: University Press of America.

Buzan Barry, 1983, *People, States and Fear: The National Security Problem in International Relations*, Wheatsheaf Books Ltd.

Buzan, B., Ole Waever, Jaap de Wilde, eds., 1998, *Security: A New Framework For Analysis*, Boulder and London: Lynne Rienner.

Davies, V. A.B, 2001, 'The Political Economy of African Civil Wars', Paper presented at the 13th Biennial Congress of the African Association of Political Science, Yaounde, Cameroon, June 19–22.

Deutsch, W. Karl, 1957, *Political Community and the North Atlantic Area: International Organizations in the Light of Historical Experience*, Princeton: Princeton University Press.

Diop, A. Y., 2000, 'Côte d'Ivoire: Learning From Democracy', *The West African Bulletin*, ECOWAS, No.8, December.

Dougherty, J.E. and Pfaltgrat, Robert (Jnr.), 1981, *Contending Theories of International Relations: A Comprehensive Survey*, Second Ed., New York: Harper and Row.

Duffield, M., 1999, 'Globalization and War Economies: Promoting Order or the Return of History', *The Fletcher Forum of World Affairs*, Vol.23, No.2, Fall.

El-Ayouty, Y. and Zartman, W., eds., 1984, *The OAU After Twenty Years*, New York: Preager Publishers.

Ellis, S., 1998, 'Liberia's Warlord Insurgency', in C. Clapham (ed.), *African Guerrillas*, Oxford: James Currey.

Enzenberger, H. M., 1993, *Inbordeskrig*, Stockholm: Norstedts Storpocket.

Evans, G. and Newnham, J., 1992, *The Dictionary of World Politics*, New York: Harvester Wheatsheaf.

Evans, G., 1994, *Cooperating for Peace: The Global Agenda for the 1990s and Beyond*, Australia: Allen and Unwin.

Femmes Africa Solidarité, 1997, *Women's Participation in the Peace Process in Sierra Leone*, Switzerland: AGL FM Production.

Ferme, M., 1998, 'The Violence of Numbers: Consensus, Competition and the Negotiation of Disputes in Sierra Leone', *Cahiers d'Etudes Africaines*, 150–152, XXXVIII.

Galtung, J., 1981,'Cultural Violence', *Journal of Peace Research*, Vol.27, No.3.

Garuba, C., 1998, *Capacity Building for Crisis Management in Africa*, Lagos.

Grossman, H.I., 1991, 'Kleptocracy and Revolution', *Oxford Economic Papers*, 51.

Hampson, F., 1990, 'Building a Stable Peace: Opportunities and Limits to Security in Third World Regional Conflicts', *International Journal*, XLV, 2, spring.

Hay, R., 1999, *Peace-building during Peace Support Operations: A Survey and Analysis of Recent Missions*, Canada, Department of Foreign Affairs of International Trade, March 14.

Herkovits, J., 1998, 'Africans Solving African Problems: Militaries, Democracies, and Security in West and Southern Africa', Report of a Conference on sub-Saharan Africa Security Project, New York.

Howe, H., 1997, 'Lessons of Liberia: ECOMOG and Regional Peacekeeping', in E. Michael et al. (eds.), *Nationalism and Ethnic Conflict*, Cambridge: The MIT Press.

Human Rights Watch/Africa, 1994, *Easy Prey: Child Soldiers in Liberia*.

Hurbert, D., 1999, 'Human Security: Safety for People in a Changing World', Paper presented at the Two-Day Regional Conference on the Management of African Security and Challenges of the 21st Century, Nigerian Institute of International Affairs and the Canadian High Commission, Lagos, June 23–24.

Hyden, G., 2000, 'Post-War Reconstruction and Democratization: Concepts, Goals and Lessons Learnt', Paper prepared for the seminar on After war: Reconciliation and Democratization in Divided Societies, Solstrand, 27-29 March.

Imobighe, T.A, 1993, 'Security in Sub-Saharan Africa', J. Singh and Bernauer T. (eds.), *Security of Third World Countries*, United Nations Institute for Disarmament Research (UNIDIR), Partmouth Publishing Company.

Imobighe T.A, 2005, 'Exploring the Conflict Management Potentials and Capacity of the AU Peace and Security Council', Paper Presented at the One Day National

Conference on the African Union and the Future of the African Continent, Nigerian Institute of International Affairs, Lagos, January 13.

Isard, W., 2000, 'Formative and Early Years of the Peace Science Society (International)', *Conflict Management and Peace Science*, Vol.18, No.1.

Joseph, R., 1987, *Democracy and Prebendal Politics in Nigeria: The Rise and Fall of the Second Republic*, Cambridge: Cambridge University Press.

Keen, D., 1998, 'The Political Economy of War', Workshop on Economic and Social Consequences of Conflicts, Queen Elizabeth House, University of Oxford.

Kivimaki, T. & Laakso, L. eds., 2000, *Greed, Grievance and Weak States: Overview of African Conflicts*, Helsinki: Department of Political Science and Department of Development Studies.

Kumar, Chetan, 1998, *Building Peace in Haiti*, New York, International Peace Academy, Occasional Paper.

Jeune Afrique, 2000, January.

Lederach, J.P., 1997, *Building Peace: Sustainable Reconciliation in Divided Societies*, Washington D.C.: United States Institute of Peace, p.75.

Mackinlay, J., ed., 1996, *A Guide to Peace Support Operations*, Providence: R.I. Brown University, Thomas J. Watson Jnr. Institute for International Studies.

Maiese, M., 2003, *What it Means to Build a Lasting Peace*, Colorado: University of Colorado, Conflict Research Consortium.

Martin, S., 'Concept of Peace remains Elusive for many Children', *APA Monitor*, Vol.29, No.10, October.

Mbu, M., 1997, 'A Reappraisal of Nigeria's Foreign Policy', *Emwai Centre for Political and Economic Research Journal*, Vol.5, No.2.

Michaud, P., 2000, 'Guei, I'm the man', *New African*, No.358, September.

Miller, R. and Necla Tschirgi, 2003, *Canada and Missions of Peace*, Ottawa: IDRC.

Mkandawire, T., 2002, 'The Terrible Toll of Post Colonial 'rebel movements' in Africa: Towards an Explanation of the Violence Against Peasantry', *Journal of Modern African Studies*, Vol.40, No.2.

Molam, M. et.al., 2002, *Peacekeeping in Sierra Leone: UNAMSIL Hits the Home Front*, Pretoria: Institute of Security Studies.

Moller, B., 2001, *Conflict Prevention and Peace-Building in Africa*, Copenhagen: Copenhagen Peace Research Institute, working papers 28/.

Mutisya, G., 1998, 'Conflict Watch', *Conflict Trends*, No.5, October.

Muyangwa, M. and Vogt, M. A. eds, 2000, *An Assessment of the OAU Mechanism for Conflict Prevention, Management and Resolution, 1993 – 2000*, New York: International Peace Academy, November.

Namadi, M. M., 2000, 'The Concept of Peace Culture and Education for Peace Building', Paper presented at the Sub-Regional Seminar on the Perspectives of Peace Education as a Basis for Achieving as Culture of Peace in Africa, Nigerian National Commission for UNESCO, August 15-17, Abuja.

Nkiwane, T., 2001,'The Future of Peace Keeping in Africa', *Africa Insight*, Vol.30, Nos.3-4 January.

NIIA, 1999, Communiqué of the Regional Conference on The Management of African Security In The 21st Century, Nigerian Institute of International Affairs, Lagos, Nigeria, 23-24 June.

Nwokedi, E., 1996, African Security: Issues and Problems in the 1990s to the Next Millennium', Margaret Vogt and L.S. Aminu (eds), *PeaceKeeping as a Security Strategy in Africa: Chad and Liberia as Case Studies*, Enugu: Fourth Dimension Publishers.

Nwokedi, E., 1999, 'Extra-African Conflict Management Initiatives and African Security', Paper read at the Regional Conference on The Management of African Security in the 21st Century, Nigerian Institute of International Affairs, Lagos, 23–24 June.

Nwolise, O.B.C, 2004, 'Traditional Approaches to Conflict Resolution Among the Igbo People of Nigeria: Reinforcing the Need for Africa to Rediscover its Roots', *AMANI Journal of African Peace*, Vol.1, No.1.

Oche, O., 2004, 'The Commonwealth and the Imperatives of Conflict Management and Human Security', *Nigerian Journal of International Affairs*, Vol.30, No.2.

Ochoche, S.A, 2000, 'Conflict Resolution and Prevention in West Africa: The Role of Education for Tolerance and a Culture of Peace', Paper presented at the Sub-Regional Seminar on The Perspectives of Education for Tolerance as a Basis for Achieving a Culture of Peace in Africa, Organised by the Nigerian National Commission for UNASCO, 15 – 17 August, ECOWAS Secretariat, Abuja.

OAU, 1996, 'Resolving Conflicts', *OAU Conflict Management Bulletin*, Vol.1, No.6, October – November.

OAU, 2000, Constitutive Act of the African Union, Lome, Togo, 12 June.

Ogwu, S. O., 1994, 'Nigeria and the Liberian Imbroglio: An Epitome of Nigeria-led Crisis Resolution in the Sub-Region', *Nigerian Forum*, Vol.13, Nos.9-10, September-October.

Olukoshi, A. and Laakso, L., eds., 1996, *Challenges to the Nation-State in Africa*, Institute of Development Studies, University of Helsinki, Helsinki.

Omunizua, C., 2000, 'Democracy or "democrazy"', *West Africa*, 16-22 October.

Peters, J., 1999, 'The Nature of African Conflicts', Paper presented at the Regional Conference on the Management of African Security in the 21st Century, Nigerian Institute of International Affairs, Lagos, 23-24 June.

Rake, A., 'Will Peace Hold?', *New African*, No.366, September.

Reno, W., 1998, *Warlord Politics and African States*, Boulder Co.: Lynne Rienner.

Reno, W., 2001, *Sierra Leone: Diamonds and the Struggle for Democracy*, London, International Peace Academy Occasional Paper Series Boulder Co., Lynne Rienner Publishers, p.175.

Renda, L., 1999, 'Ending Civil Wars: The Case of Liberia', *The Fletcher Forum of World Affairs*, Vol.23: 2.

Reychler, L., 1994, 'The Art of Conflict Prevention: Theory and Practice', in W. Bauwens and L. Reychler (eds.), *The Art of Conflict Prevention*, London: Brassey's.

Reychler, L., 2001, 'From Conflict to Sustainable Peace-building: Concepts and Analytical Tools', Luc Reychler and Thania Paffenholz (eds.), *Peace-building: A Field Guide*, Boulder, Colorado: Lynne Rienner Publishers, p.12.

Richards P., 1996, *Fighting for the Rainforest: War, Youth and Resources in Sierra Leone*, London: James Currey.

Seck, J., 2000, *West Africa Small Arms Moratorium: High Level Consultations on the Modalities for the Implementation of PCASED*, United Nations Institute for Disarmament Research (UNIDIR), Geneva, and the United Nations Regional Centre for Peace and Disarmament in Africa (UNRCPDA), Lome, Togo, February.

Schuster, L., 1994, 'The Final Days of Dr. Doe', *Granta*, No.48, summer.

Sklar, R.L., 1991, 'Peace Through Freedom: The Resolution of International Conflict in Sub-Saharan Africa', Paper presented at the International Conference on Regional Conflict and Diplomatic Initiatives, Nigerian Institute of International Affairs, Lagos, Nigeria, 12-31, October.

Slack, A. and Doyon, Roy, R., 2001,'Population Dynamics and Susceptibility for Ethnic Conflict: The Case of Bosnia and Herzegovina', *Journal of Peace Research*, Vol.38, No.2.

Stedman, S., 1991, 'Conflict and Conflict Resolution in Africa: A Conceptual Framework', Francis Deng and I. William Zartman (eds.), *Conflict Resolution in Africa*, Washington D.C.: The Brookings Institute.

Stephens, K., 1997, 'Building Peace in Deeply Rooted Conflicts: Exploring New Ideas to shape the Future', International Understanding Conference, INCORE, January.

The West African Bulletin, 1999, 'Farewell to Arms in Liberia', No.7, October.

UNDP, 1994, *Human Development Report*, Geneva.

UNDP, 1999, 'Globalization with a Human Face', *Human Development Report*, Geneva.

Umar-Omole, P., 2001, 'Obasanjo, Konare, Kabbah Hail Truce in Sierra Leone', *THISDAY Newspaper* (Nigeria), Vol.7, No.2299.

UNESCO, 1999, 'Global Movement for a Culture of Peace and Non-Violence', CAB-WS/4.

United Nations, 1998, The Causes of Conflict and the Promotion of Durable Peace and Sustainable Development in Africa, Report of the Secretary-General to the United Nations Security Council, 16 April.

United Nations, 1996, *United Nations' Peace Keeping*, New York: UN Department of Public Information.

UN Document S/1998/825, Annex I, Ceasefire agreement in Guinea-Bissau, I September 1998, Article I(d).

UN Document S/1999/432, Annex, *Report on the Situation in Guinea-Bissau prepared by the Executive Secretary of ECOWAS*, 16 April 1999, para.8.

UNRISD, 1995, *States of Disarray: The Social Effects of Globalization*, Geneva.

'Uprising in Guinea-Bissau', *Africa Research Bulletin*, Vol.35, No.6, 1-30 June, 1998.

Vajpeyi, K., 1997 'Paradox of Peace', Available online: www.lifepositive.com/mind/ethics-and-values/peace/peace-value.asp.

Vogt, M.A., ed., 1992, *The Liberian Crisis and ECOMOG: A Bold Attempt at Regional Peacekeeping*, Lagos: Gabuma Publishing Co.

Vogt, M.A and Aminu, L.S., eds., 1996, *Peacekeeping as a Security Strategy in Africa: Chad and Liberia as Case Studies*, 2 vols., Enugu: Fourth Dimension Publishing Co.

Weeks, D., 1992, *The Eight Essential Steps to Conflict Resolution*, New York: Tarcher/Putman.

Wilkinson, P., 1998, 'Sharpening the Weapons of Peace Support Operations and Complex Emergencies', *Peace Keeping and Conflict Resolution*.

Young, C., 1988, 'The African Colonial State and Its Political Legacy', in D. Rothchild and N. Chazan (eds.) *The Precarious Balance: The State and Security in Africa*, Boulder, Colorado: Westview Press.

Zack-Williams, A. B, 'Sierra Leone: The Political Economy of Civil War, 1991–98', *Third World Quarterly*, Vol. 20, No.1.

Zartman I.W., 1995, *Collapsed States: The Disintegration and Restoration of Legitimate Authority*, Boulder Co.: Lynne Reinner.